STARSTRUCK

Rachna Chhabria is a versatile writer who has worked as a creative writing teacher, blogger, columnist and freelance writer for various English newspapers. She enjoys writing quirky characters who take her on crazy adventures. Her forte is creative non-fiction and fantasy. She also loves writing animal stories. She is a prize-winning author and many of her books are bestsellers. Her short stories are a part of several school textbooks. Some of her notable works include *Amazing Creatures: The A to Z of Animals, Birds and Insects*; *Banku's Terrific Tails*; *Neev and Buddha*; *Jai and the Vegetable Superheroes*; *Ganesha's Gifts*; *Vocabulary Villa*; *Shiva and Parvati in Magadhpur*; *The Giggling Girl*; *50 GREAT INDIANS: Extraordinary Lives, Inspiring Tales*; *Festival Stories Through the Year* and *Lazy Worm Goes on a Journey.*

STARSTRUCK

Stories of the Nakshatras in the Sky

RACHNA CHHABRIA

Illustrated by Vibha Surya

hachette INDIA

First published in paperback in 2025 by Hachette India
(Registered name: Hachette Book Publishing India Pvt. Ltd)
An Hachette UK company
www.hachetteindia.com

1

ISBN 978-93-5731-515-9

Hachette Book Publishing India Pvt. Ltd
4th & 5th Floors, Corporate Centre
Plot No. 94, Sector 44, Gurugram – 122003, India

Typeset by Manmohan Kumar, Delhi

MIX
Paper | Supporting responsible forestry
FSC® C010615
www.fsc.org

Printed and bound in India
by Thomson Press India Ltd.

For my Guru,
Sadguru Mata Amritanandamayi Devi (Amma)
Grace, Blessings and Intuition

CONTENTS

INTRODUCTION

Since ancient times, stars have fascinated humankind. The ancient seers who first observed and wrote about these stars had no instruments. They trusted their intuition and wisdom that came from their prayers and penances. They believed that these stars were special; that they held powers, and could influence many aspects of our lives. This unwavering belief laid the foundation for Vedic astrology – an ancient system of knowledge rooted in the movement of celestial bodies known as nakshatras. Pronounced as 'nuk-shuh-tras,' the word *nakshatra* is made of two words – *naksha*, meaning 'map,' and *tara*, meaning 'star.' So *nakshatra* means 'map of stars,' or 'mapping of a person's stars.'

The word *nakshatra* carries a sense of beauty, a shroud of mystery, and a quiet power. It feels ancient and layered, wrapped in meanings that are not immediately obvious. It is a system of twenty-seven distinct star clusters forming unique patterns across the sky. Often referred to as 'lunar mansions,' these twenty-seven nakshatras are central to

Vedic astrology – a system of knowledge that dates back thousands of years. While most of us are familiar with sun signs or the twelve zodiac signs, Vedic astrology places great importance on the moon sign, known as the Janma Nakshatra – the star under which a person is born.

Let us now return to explore what these 'lunar mansions' of the Moon really are. Why are they called lunar mansions? It is because the moon lives in each house or a mansion for a day and a night in a sidereal lunar month or the sidereal cycle of the moon. In Hindu scriptures, these twenty-seven nakshatras are the daughters of Prajapati Daksha and his wife, Asikni. These bright, twinkling queens of the night sky are all married to Chandra, the handsome Moon god, making him spend equal time with each wife. Some believe that there are twenty-eight nakshatras. The last one, Abhijit, is supposedly invisible.

Let me clarify that the order of the nakshatras has nothing to do with the power and status of any nakshatra. Like all the numbers are equally important, but just come one after another, likewise for the nakshatras.

Since the moon plays an important part in astrology, astrologers pay close attention to its position at the time of a person's birth. Simply put, they look at which star was the moon aligned to at the moment of birth. When a child is born, the date, time, and place of birth are carefully noted. Using these details, an astrologer prepares the person's birth chart – popularly known as horoscope – seen as a kind of map of life's possibilities. This astrological chart reflects the position of the nakshatras at birth and tracks how these stars move and shift over time. From this, astrologers say they can glimpse hints about a person's path – career, relationships, health, work, and other aspects – while offering guidance to navigate their life.

Let's discuss why these nakshatras are so important. For those who follow these beliefs, these stars, these distant points of brightness and light, are believed to cast a quiet influence over a person's journey. They are believed to hold clues about a person's nature, personality, skills, traits, behaviour, and even hints to the path or paths the person will take in life, the obstacles, and problems they encounter in their lifetime.

Doesn't the world of nakshatras sound both exciting and fascinating? It makes you want to know more, doesn't it? And perhaps, right now, there's one burning question racing through your mind: Will I score well in my exams? Will I win that race? Will I crack the engineering entrance test?

Well, here's the truth – the nakshatras won't give you the answers to those questions. Your result depends on your hard work and preparation. These are all things that you shouldn't bother the nakshatras with. What the nakshatras can do, though, is help you understand yourself better – your tendencies, your strengths, and how you respond to challenges. Think of them as a guiding map, not a shortcut.

Each nakshatra is said to carry a power, an energy, which is known as shakti (not to be confused with the goddess Shakti), and this is the power of the deity (devata) presiding over that particular nakshatra. Many believe that the personality of this divine guardian leaves its imprint on the nakshatra, and that those born under it may, in some mysterious way, carry a trace of that cosmic character. Think of it as a cosmic DNA – much like you might have your father's smile, your mother's eyes, or your grandmother's dimples.

For those who follow such beliefs, knowing which nakshatras guide them can offer a sense of direction. The unexpected googlies can be dodged, and the tricky dot balls can be played with confidence. While the stars may whisper, at the heart of it, determination can overpower destiny. All said and done, a person is the master of their destiny. A lot depends on their determination, their faith in themselves, and their ability to triumph over all odds.

Vedic astrology associated each of these nakshatras to a planet, a deity, some symbols, and a sage. All of us have, at some point, looked up at the dazzling night sky and wondered about those bright, twinkling stars. As children, we heard all kinds of stories about them – magical, mysterious tales passed down through generations. Later, in school, our teachers and textbooks offered a different, more scientific version of the story.

Now, it is time to discover another layer – the world of the nakshatras, their planets, their sages, and the deities they are linked to. So, what are we waiting for? Let's dive into the fascinating world of these celestial stars and their deities, the curses they endured, and the boons bestowed on them.

1

ASHVINI NAKSHATRA

Deity: Ashvini Kumaras, *Twin Gods of Healing*

Ashvini (also spelled as Ashwini) is the first nakshatra, not because the nakshatra's name starts with the alphabet *a*. That's just a coincidence. The word *ashvini* comes from the word *asvah*, which means 'a horse' in Sanskrit. According to some, the word *ashvini* translates to 'born of a female horse,' or 'horse-woman.' Ashvini also has another name – Asvayuj, meaning 'she who yokes horses.'

Horses were an essential part of society during the Vedic period. Kings and warriors had their favourite horses, riding them they won battles and wars. *Ratha*s, or horse-drawn chariots, were considered crucial in the military strategy and warfare. Did you know that in the Kurukshetra War all the *maharathi*s (the Pandavas, Kauravas, acharyas, and other kings) had their own chariots and charioteers?

The symbol of Ashvini nakshatra is a horse's head. Ancient Vedic seers, in the absence of telescopes and other astronomical instruments, relied solely on their naked-eye observations. When they saw the two bright stars that represent this nakshatra, their mind's eye identified a pattern – it resembled the head of a horse. Easily visible in the night sky, these two bright stars are Gamma Arietis and Beta Arietis. Both these stars are used for navigation. They lie below the Andromeda constellation (named after Princess Andromeda in Greek mythology).

Just like we have one or two pet names and a formal name, similarly, stars have multiple names and designations. Gamma Arietis is also known as Mesarthim and Beta Arietis as Sheratan. As Ashvini nakshatra occupies the space from 0°00' to 13°20' (the first 13 degrees and 20 minutes) of the zodiac sign Aries, it gets slotted as the first nakshatra, heralding the start of the astrological cycle.

The ruling planet of this nakshatra is Ketu (South Lunar Node). Personified as a deity, Ketu is one part of the immortal *asura* (demon) Svarbhanu, who disguised himself as a deva and secretly partook the *amrita*, nectar of immortality, during the Samudra Manthan (also known as Amrita Manthan or Sagar Manthan, it was the churning of the ocean of milk by the devas and asuras to get amrita, the elixir of eternal life). Svarbhanu was hiding between Surya (the Sun god) and Chandra (the Moon god), and when his trick came to light, Lord Vishnu beheaded him with his Sudarshan Chakra. As he had already consumed some nectar and become immortal, the asura's head became Rahu and his body became Ketu. Rahu is known as the North Lunar Node and Ketu as the South Lunar Node.

Marichi is the rishi associated with this nakshatra. Marichi is the father of the famous Rishi Kashyapa and the grandfather of the devas (gods) and asuras (demons). That sure makes him powerful and a well-known name in the world of rishis.

There is another symbol associated with this nakshatra – two horses drawing a chariot in which two people are seated. This points to the two deities of this nakshatra, the Ashvini Kumaras – Nasatya and Dasra. Radiant and youthful, these divine twins ride a golden chariot drawn by galloping horses, symbolizing speed. It must have been a sight to behold, don't you think?

The elder twin, Nasatya, was considered the god of health and the younger brother, Dasra, was the god of medicine. They are depicted as celestial physicians in Hindu mythology and are believed to dispel illnesses and ill fate and bring health and wellness to their worshipers.

Now, let's learn the story of their birth as described in the Vishnu Purana. The Ashvini Kumaras were born to Surya (also known as Vivasvan) and his wife, Sanjana (also known as Samjana, which means consciousness, or Saranyu). Surya and Sanjana were a happy couple. They had three children: Manu, the first human and the father of all humans; Yama, the lord of Death; and his twin sister, Yami, also known as River Yamuna.

But there was a small problem. Sanjana was unable to tolerate Surya's intense heat. Imagine being that close to the sun. She was getting drained of energy. So, she created a mirror image of herself, her shadow, called Chhaya. Instructing her to remain with Surya, Sanjana retreated to earth. She took on the guise of a mare and lived in the forest, performing penance.

Meanwhile, Surya, unaware that his wife was missing, had three children with Chhaya. They were Shani, the deity of planet Saturn, another Manu, and Tapati (goddess of River Tapti). Chhaya and Surya were happy. But Chhaya became partial to her children and started ignoring Sanjana's children. This treatment didn't affect Sanjana's son Manu, but it irritated Yama. One day, an angry Yama lifted his foot to kick Chhaya. The moment he realized what he was doing, he immediately dropped his foot. But Chhaya had seen that action. Furious, she cursed Yama that as he had lifted his foot to kick her, the same foot would get infested with maggots and drop away from his body.

Surya heard the curse. He immediately felt that something wasn't right. Sanjana was a kind mother and she wouldn't curse her son, no matter how much he troubled her. This is when Surya realized that this woman living with him as his wife wasn't actually his wife.

When Surya confronted Chhaya, she could not keep the secret and blurted out the entire story. Through his powers, Surya realized that Sanjana was meditating in the forest, disguised as a mare. Transforming into a stallion, he approached Sanjana in the forest.

Recognizing her husband in disguise, Sanjana tried to escape. But Surya soon caught her and convinced her

Surya later tweaked this curse by changing the words, so that instead of the foot falling away, the flesh-eating maggots fell away. But sadly, by then, Yama's foot had suffered some damage and earned him the name of Sirnapada, meaning 'the one with the shrivelled foot.'

to stay. The stallion (Surya) and the mare (Sanjana) had three more children, the Ashvini Kumara twins and a son named Revanta. The twins were born from each nostril of their mother, the mare. Later, Surya brought his wife back to his abode.

The Ashvini Kumaras were highly revered. They are mentioned 376 times in the Rig Veda (one of the four sacred texts of Hindus) and have 57 hymns dedicated to them. Firm believers in the power of Ayurveda, they were the original brand ambassadors of the ancient Indian system of medicine. Their ability to bring the dead back to life made these two ever-youthful brothers popular deities.

These wily brothers also used their medical skills to their advantage. Indra, considered in the Vedas as the king of the gods and ruler of heaven, was the only deity possessing the knowledge of how to brew Soma, the much sought-after elixir of immortality. Though possessive

The Ashvini Kumara twins have a Mahabharata connection. Queen Madri, the second wife of King Pandu, invoked the Ashvini Kumaras and was blessed with twins Nakul and Sahadeva. This makes them the spiritual fathers of Nakul and Sahadeva, the youngest of the five Pandava brothers. Nakul was a skilled horseman and Sahadeva was known for his intellect and knowledge of astrology.

of this knowledge, he passed this information to the powerful sage Dadhichi as he was certain it would be safe in the renowned sage's hands. But still insecure, Indra added a curse so it wouldn't get into the wrong hands and be misused. He cursed Dadhichi that if he shared this information with anyone else, his head would fall off. Assured that the secret of Soma was safe with Dadhichi, Indra taught the sage knowledge of other herbs, too.

The Ashvini Kumara twins were eager to learn this secret. With their knowledge of surgical skills, they switched Dadhichi's head with that of a horse. Now Dadhichi had no problem sharing the soma recipe through the horse's mouth. After learning the secret from the horse's mouth, the twins conveniently swapped the horse head back with Dadhichi's head.

Indra, though furious, was helpless as Dadhichi had kept his word and sealed his lips. It was the head of the horse who had blabbered away all the secrets.

These celestial physicians were big-time cheerleaders of the underdogs. The brothers saved the smaller animals by whisking them away when they were on the verge of being gobbled up by the larger ones. Going a step further, they healed the animals of the diseases afflicting them.

POPULAR BELIEFS

People born under this nakshatra are self-sufficient and resourceful. They will somehow find a solution to any problem they face. So, if you were born under this nakshatra, you would definitely know how to get out of the most tedious job around the house that your parents have given you. All courtesy the quick-thinking Ashvini Kumara twins who will be mentoring you all along the way, and also due to your own creative and quick thinking.

There is so much to learn from the Ashvini Kumara twins, their quick-thinking nature and healing tendencies and their ability to look out for unique solutions to problems is an asset that comes in handy in difficult times and situations.

2

BHARANI NAKSHATRA

Deity: Yama, *The Guardian of Justice*

It does look like the list of nakshatras is following the alphabetical order, the second nakshatra being Bharani. But it is another coincidence. The name *bharani* comes from the Sanskrit word *bharana*, which means 'to bear,' 'to carry,' or 'she who bears.'

This nakshatra is represented by three faint stars in the Aries constellation: 35 Arietis, 39 Arietis, and 41 Arietis. Ancient Vedic seers saw these stars forming a triangle in the night sky. To them, this triangle appeared symbolic of *yoni* – a sacred representation of the feminine life-giving force in Vedic tradition.

To many ancient civilizations and cultures, women's ability to reproduce represented the fertile aspect of nature. Nature itself was considered a female and addressed as 'Mother Nature.'

There is another symbol of this nakshatra: a boat. Just like a boat transports people from one place to another, the womb transfers a soul from the spirit plane to the physical world.

Venus (Shukra) is the ruling planet of this nakshatra. The brightest of all planets and far more radiant than any of the stars, Venus is called the 'morning star' as well as the 'evening star.' Two interesting facts: first, Venus glows with a silver light that is steady, unlike the stars that twinkle; and second, it moves from the eastern horizon in the early morning to the western sky in the early evening. For ancient farmers and shepherds, this predictable pattern helped them to guide their flock, thus earning the title of 'The Shepherd's Star.'

Vashishta is the rishi associated with this nakshatra. One of the most revered and powerful sages, he was Rama's and his brothers' teacher, as well as their family priest.

The deity of this nakshatra is Yama, the god of death. He is one of the most feared gods in Hinduism. A powerful and just deity, he oversees the transition of souls and upholds cosmic law. When he arrives riding a buffalo, his large, red eyes glowering, clad in red robes, his dark skin shining, fear ripples down peoples' spines. One quick glance at the mace or the stick (*Kaldanda*) and the noose in his hands and people get nervous.

Yama's association with Bharani reflects the nakshatra's deep connection to life, death, and transformation. The noose in his hand signifies the souls Yama lassoes into his control. This soul-capturing attribute has given him the name of 'Pasi,' the noose carrier. According to the Rig Veda, he also has two insatiable hounds. These four-eyed dogs trail him and guard the path the dead take in the afterlife to reach Yama's abode Yamapura, or Yamloka, deep in the belly of the earth, in the underworld. It is believed that sometimes these two hounds visit the world of the living to search for souls or to beckon them to Yama's palace. Imagine walking down a busy road with your friends and bumping into two four-eyes dogs. It wouldn't be long before you turn around and run, just in case the dogs start chasing you!

For all the fear Yama evoked in people, there was one boy who stood tall against the god of death. The Padma Purana narrates this beautiful story. A long, long time ago, sage Mrikandu and his wife, Marudvati, prayed to Lord Shiva for a child and received a son as a blessing. While this son, named Markandeya, would be virtuous, he would only live to be sixteen. When the young boy turned fifteen, he came to know that he was destined to die on his sixteenth birthday. To escape this dreadful fate awaiting him, young Markandeya started meditating and praying to Lord Shiva by sitting in front of a *lingam*, a symbol of Shiva.

On his sixteenth birthday, Yamadutas, the messengers of Yama, arrived to take his soul. But they couldn't even go near the boy as he had acquired a lot of spiritual power with his meditation. They returned to the lord of death empty-handed. Yama decided that he would go and get the boy himself. Carrying his noose in his hand, he arrived at the place the boy was meditating. When Yama threw the noose around the boy to capture him, the boy immediately sprang up and hugged the lingam, crying for mercy. As the noose was now wrapped around both the boy and the lingam, a furious Shiva emerged from the lingam with his trident in hand. Everyone knows what happens when Shiva gets angry. He killed Yama and granted immortality to Markandeya.

The death of Yama worried the gods. How would the world work without him? No one would die. This wasn't right. Imagine the burden on earth if people weren't dying. The gods pleaded with Shiva, and he relented and brought Yama back to life.

You surely want to know the mantra the young boy meditated on, right? It was none other than the Maha Mrityunjaya Mantra – the triumph-over-death mantra.

Want to learn this powerful and sacred mantra?

Aum tryambakam yajaamahe sugandhim pushtivardhanam |
Urvaarukamiva bandhanaan mrityormuksheeya maamritaat ||

Meaning: We worship the three-eyed One (Shiva), who is fragrant and nourishes all. Just like a ripened cucumber falls easily from the vine to which it is attached, may we be liberated from death and the darkness of ignorance and realize our immortal selves.

In Hindu tradition, whenever someone is serious or critical in the hospital, family members either chant the Maha Mrityunjaya Mantra or get it chanted by priests in the temples. There is a Maha Mrityunjaya Homa too, a powerful Vedic fire ritual, performed to invoke Shiva's blessings to prevent untimely death.

Yama comes from an illustrious family. He is the son of Surya, the Sun god, and Sanjana, the daughter of

Vishwakarma. According to a story in the Markandeya Purana, Surya's brightness once made his pregnant wife, Sanjana, close her eyes. This angered Surya, and he cursed the twins she would give birth to, saying that as she had closed her eyes the moment he looked at her, she would give birth to Yama, the destroyer of creatures. Sanjana started trembling with fear. This brought on another curse – she would give birth to a daughter who would never be still. The boy Yama became the god of death, and the girl child was Yami, the river Yamuna.

There is another story about Yama in the Mahabharata. Once Yama had assumed the post of a chief priest in a ritual that went on for many years. As this priestly duty claimed Yama's full attention, he started neglecting his own duties as the god of death. What ensued was a complete imbalance in the world. No one was dying. All the gods appealed to Yama to resume his duties. Brought back to the realization of the job he had ignored, Yama resumed his work as the god of death. After that, order was restored in the world.

Whew! Just imagine living for centuries. That's as scary a thought as death!

POPULAR BELIEFS

People born under this nakshatra are strong and resilient, they can withstand all the turbulences life throws their way. Though, sometimes they will cry and indulge in bouts of self-pity, they will bounce back hard, just like a rubber ball. No circumstances, however trying and insurmountable they may be, can hold them down for too long. This tenacity reflects the nature of Yama – nothing can keep him at bay once he sets off on his mission to claim a soul.

Though Yama has an important role to play, he has been entrusted with a task that must have been loathed by the other gods. Nonetheless, he has performed his duty with sincerity. This shows that where duties are concerned, however good or bad, even the gods couldn't shirk responsibility.

3

KRITTIKA NAKSHATRA

Deity: Agni, *The God with Seven Tongues*

Don't let the sweet-sounding name mislead you. Krittika, the third nakshatra, has a powerful meaning that might scare people. Krittika translates to 'one who cuts,' or 'the cutter.' This nakshatra is related to the seven Krittikas – wives of the seven great sages, also known as the Saptarishis, who look after the well-being of this universe. The main symbol of this nakshatra is a sharp instrument, like an axe or a razor or a knife. A flame and a peacock are two other symbols associated with this nakshatra.

The Krittika nakshatra is represented in the sky by a group of seven bright stars huddled together in the Pleiades, a cluster of more than one thousand stars in the Taurus constellation. The Pleiades are also known as the Seven Sisters and the Messier 45 (M45).

What pattern do you think our ancient sages saw when they looked up at these seven bright stars in the night sky? Need a hint? Situated close to each other, they are strikingly radiant. It was a necklace. Now, does that give you an idea of how pretty the Pleiades cluster must be?

The scientific names of the seven beauties in the cluster are: Eta Tauri, 21 Tauri, 16 Tauri, 17 Tauri, 20 Tauri, 23 Tauri, and 19 Tauri. As per Greek mythology, Eta Tauri is Alcyone, 21 Tauri is Asterope, 16 Tauri is Celaeno, 17 Tauri is Electra, 20 Tauri is Maia, 23 Tauri is Merope, and 19 Tauri is Taygeta. Alcyone is the brightest star in the cluster.

Mars (Mangal) is the ruling planet of this nakshatra. This second-smallest planet of the solar system is also called the 'Red Planet,' as its surface is orange-red due to the iron oxide dust covering it. Because of this red colour, Mars can be easily spotted in the night sky.

The rishi associated with this nakshatra is Angiras. He is considered a mediator between gods and men. Some religious texts regard him as the first of the fire gods, who are also known as Agni Devas. Angiras is credited with the discovery of fire.

The deity of this nakshatra is Agni, the god of fire. According to the Agni Purana, Agni was the son of Rishi Angiras. Without this god, there would be no cooked food on our table, and we would be eating raw fruits and vegetables for breakfast, lunch, and dinner.

According to the story in the Puranas, Agni played an interesting role in the birth of Kartikeya, Lord Shiva's eldest son. When an immensely powerful asura called Tarakasura performed intense *tapasya*, or penance, to please Lord Brahma, he received two boons from the creator. First, no one in the three worlds could match his power; and second, only the son of Shiva could slay him. Shiva, after his wife Sati's death, had renounced the world and immersed himself in meditation. So, he was unlikely to have a child. Tarakasura was under the impression that the boons had made him nearly invincible and practically immortal. What he hadn't bargained for was that Sati would be reborn as Parvati, and through her penance she would win over Shiva and marry him.

Tarakasura went berserk after receiving the boons, creating havoc and troubling the gods and humans. Alarmed, the gods prayed to Shiva for help. Shiva answered their prayers and gave them a seed. Agni carried this seed, making his flame a womb for it. But the heat and intensity of Shiva's seed became too much for even the god of fire. When Agni felt that he couldn't tolerate this heat anymore, he placed the seed in the waters of the Ganges to protect it. It is believed that even River Ganga couldn't withstand the heat of Shiva's seed, and she dropped it into a forest of reeds, far away from prying eyes.

All the gods then made a request to the six Krittikas (wives who had been banished by their husbands, the six great sages, who believed the women had been unfaithful) to take care of the baby. The six Krittikas nursed the baby, ensuring his safety from the asuras. As they fed the baby, he split or cloned himself into six forms (this is the reason he is also known as Shanmukha, or the god with six faces), so that he could feed from all his foster mothers at the same time. That's the story of Kartikeya's birth. Isn't it interesting how the god's name is reminiscent of his foster mothers?

Agni is portrayed as a two-headed god. One head signifies immortality and the other is a symbol of life. When one sees this red-skinned deity (the colour of the skin is due to the intense heat of his persona) riding on his ram – sometimes he sits on a chariot pulled by rams or horses – it makes for a fierce sight. Agni's three legs and seven hands make him stand out from the other gods. These oddities add to his charm. As do his golden teeth and seven tongues.

Agni has a fondness for the number seven – besides having seven tongues, seven rays of light emerge from his body, signifying his fiery power. The reason for this deity's seven tongues is that he needs them to devour the ghee and other offerings made to him and the gods who are being worshipped in the yagnas.

Agni was a powerful god, and, along with Indra and Varuna, was considered the holy trinity of the Vedic times. He was also the messenger of the gods, the link between heaven and earth, the bridge between the deities and the people. That's why all yagnas require the presence of Agni, the sacrificial fire. He was so revered during the Vedic times that over 200 hymns in his honour occupy prime space in the Rig Veda, with eight out of the ten books starting with hymns in praise of Agni.

Agni's wife is Svaha, or Swaha. You must have heard it being chanted while an offering is made to the fire. Swaha

Agni resides in three spaces: on earth in the form of fire, in mid space as lightning, and in heaven as the sun.

Did you know that we have agni in our bodies, too? If there was no agni, we wouldn't be able to digest our food. This agni is the digestive power in our body.

was in love with Agni and did a lot to win his affection. Their bond was so strong that Agni ended up ensuring that sacrificial offerings to him should be accompanied by his wife's name.

POPULAR BELIEFS

People born under this nakshatra have resolute willpower. So, if you were born under this nakshatra, no amount of distraction could take you away from the task at hand – be it homework or any other project. This strong willpower, courage, and the ability to remain undistracted is derived from Agni. Because once a fire starts, it is undistracted in its mission and it takes a lot of effort to control it. People born under this star also like to call a spade a spade. This can prove to be a bit of a problem as sometimes even a spade doesn't want to be told the truth.

There are so many facets to Agni's personality. He can nourish and provide warmth as well as destroy and cause havoc. He can be as gentle as a fire crackling in the fireplace, warming you up on a cold winter night, he can also be the slow flame simmering one's meals and keeping them hot. He is the scary bolt of lightning in the sky, and he is also the raging fire burning everything in its path.

4

ROHINI NAKSHATRA

Deity: Brahma, *Creator of the Universe*

Rohini, a popular feminine name, is the fourth nakshatra. Rohini means 'the reddish one.' This nakshatra has two other names: Vidhi and Viranchi. Viranchi (or Virinchi) means Brahma.

Rohini is represented in the sky by one of the brightest stars in the Taurus constellation called the Alpha Tauri, or Aldebaran. This star has a pale rose tinge to it, and it shines with so much radiance that it can be easily spotted in the night sky. It is no wonder then that our ancient Vedic scholars and seers consider this star the abode of Brahma as well as the Prajapatis. The creator of the universe must have the most unique abode coveted by many.

The symbol of this nakshatra can be a bit puzzling. It is an ox cart pulled by two oxen. One can never figure out how the ancient seers came up with such a symbol.

The radiant Moon (Chandra) is the ruling planet of this nakshatra. According to the Vedic seers, the mind of god manifests in the moon. The different phases of the moon, from the new moon slowly going on to the full moon and then returning back are symbolic of the cyclical nature of life, which is depicted in the different stages, namely birth, childhood, adulthood, old age, and then rebirth. Moon is supposed to be the happiest when he is with Rohini. She is his favourite consort, and she even ended up getting her husband a curse from her father, Prajapati Daksha, because of this favouritism.

Atri, one of the most powerful rishis, is associated with this nakshatra. He is also the father of the Moon god, known as Chandra deva. Atri was respected and revered for his immense wisdom and knowledge. Kings and deities sought his guidance on important matters.

Brahma, the creator of the universe, is the main deity of Rohini. From the twenty-seven nakshatras, there are just three that have one of the trinities as their main deities. Don't you think that makes Rohini a VIP nakshatra?

Entrusted with the creative aspect of nature, of the world, Brahma ensures how everything ultimately looks. From the tiniest leaf to the towering mountains, from the bubbling musical brooks to the gushing rivers, from the beautiful flowers to the pretty butterflies – everything has Brahma's creative stamp on it.

Don't you want to know how the creator came into existence? Here's the beautiful story of Brahma's birth:

In the beginning, the cosmos was just water and darkness. Into this darkness came consciousness, or Purusha, who is none other than Vishnu, reclining in the ocean, partially submerged in the water. Bubbles started emerging from his body. These bubbles were like golden eggs as Purusha was pure consciousness. Each bubble was a part of him, and his essence lay inside each egg.

As Purusha was partially submerged in the ocean, water collected in his navel, and from this water grew a beautiful lotus flower. When the lotus unfurled its petals, Brahma, the god of creation, emerged. Brahma had no idea how he had come into being, who he was, where he was, or what he was supposed to do. He looked in all directions, east, west, north, south, and he also looked up. This action gave him five heads. (Brahma lost one of his heads when he lied to Shiva. In anger, the destroyer of the Trinity cut off one of Brahma's heads, leaving him with four heads.) But all he encountered was complete silence. There were so many questions inside Brahma's mind, but no one to answer them.

In the still vastness, Purusha uttered a single word: 'Tapa.' This contained a command and an answer to all of Brahma's questions. It also held a world of meaning: be still and control yourself. Like an obedient student, Brahma did exactly that. He stilled his body and mind, making himself receptive to all the knowledge Purusha imparted him. He became like a sponge, soaking in everything from Purusha, until there was nothing more left to learn. Using all this knowledge, Brahma created the different forms of the Universe and all the creatures in it. This is the reason Brahma is called the original Prajapati.

Certain Puranas attribute Brahma's birth to having appeared from a golden egg called Hiranyagarbha, which emerged from the ocean.

Brahma is one of the few gods who doesn't hold any weapons in his hands. He has the sacred texts (the Vedas) in one hand, a *mala* (rosary) in the other hand, a lotus in the third hand, and a *kamandalu* (water pot carried by sages) in his fourth hand. All these objects are full of symbolism. The scrolls of Vedas symbolize knowledge, the mala depicts time, the lotus is associated with reality and purity, and the kamandalu points to the origin of creation from water. Brahma is usually depicted with four heads, each pointing in a different direction, four hands, and a beard. Sitting on a lotus, Brahma watches the world with his mount (*vahana*), the white swan, close to him. Some texts mention a wooden ladle (known as *sruk* or *sruva*) instead of a lotus flower

There are not many temples dedicated to the creator of the universe. The Brahma Temple at Pushkar is the most famous one. The Erawan Shrine in Bangkok, dedicated to Brahma, is a popular tourist destination and a place of worship for the Thai Buddhists.

You will be stunned to know that according to some theories, the country Burma's (now known as Myanmar) name is a derivative of Brahma. This conclusion has been arrived at because some medieval texts mention a Brahma desa, which is assumed to be Burma, because of the similarity of the two names.

in one of Brahma's hands. The ladle is used during yagna ceremonies to pour the offerings into the fire to the chant of the priest's mantras.

It is believed that Brahma's four heads also represent the four Vedas, the four yugas, the four directions, the four ashramas or stages of life, and the four varnas.

As it was Brahma's job to further create the world, he created the ten Prajapatis (the forefathers of the human race) and the seven sages known as the Saptarishis. All these children are called Brahma's Manasputras.

It is also believed that the eighth avatar of Vishnu, the eternal favourite Lord Krishna, was born under this nakshatra. Krishna's birthday, known as Krishna Janmashtami, is celebrated when the moon is in the Rohini nakshatra.

POPULAR BELIEFS

People born under this nakshatra are known for their balanced nature. No extreme emotions for them, like throwing a sulk or whooping with joy. When we see an image of Brahma, the first thought that strikes one is a god who is calm and composed. Perhaps this trait has been passed down to the people born under this nakshatra. They can also charm a bird off the tree with their gentle and persuasive nature. Just like the teacher who has given you a long list of tedious assignments for the weekend, making it look like they are giving you a treat.

Brahma's work sure wasn't easy. As the creator, he loved all his creations equally, but many went on to disobey him and make his job harder. But, despite the setbacks, his work (creation) continued.

5

MRIGASHIRA NAKSHATRA

Deity: Chandra, *Prince Charming of the Cosmic World*

The fifth nakshatra is Mrigashira. *Mriga* means deer and *shira* is head. Therefore, Mrigashira is 'deer's head.' This nakshatra has four more names: Saumya, Arghayani, Chandra, and Udupa. Saumya means 'benevolent.' This name could also be a derivative of Soma, the divine nectar. Arghayani translates to 'start of the year.' Chandra and Udupa refer to the moon. The ancient seers at times liked to complicate things.

Four stars, one bright and three faint, in the Orion constellation represent this nakshatra in the sky. The world knows the four stars as Bellatrix (Gamma Orionis), Pi^2 Orionis, Pi^3 Orionis (Tabit), and Pi^4 Orionis. Bellatrix is the brightest of this lot and the third-brightest in the constellation. It shines on the top right shoulder of Orion, with the other three stars forming the shape of a bow, tilted towards Bellatrix. When ancient seers saw this pattern, it gave them the impression of a deer's head and it became the symbol of this nakshatra.

Another symbol for Mrigashira nakshatra is a pot full of Soma (the favourite drink of the gods, like yours is a fizzy cola). This drink is considered the nectar of the celestial beings, the secret to their eternal youthful looks, and symbolizes nourishment, immortality, and rejuvenation. Soma is also linked to Chandra. While it is the Sanskrit name of Chandra, it is believed that Soma (life) is held in Chandra.

Mars, or Mangal, is the ruling planet of this nakshatra. Pulastya is the rishi associated with this nakshatra. He was one of the ten Prajapatis and is counted among the Saptarishis. It is believed that Pulastya was a member of Indra's court. He is the one who received the Vishnu Purana from Brahma and narrated it to sage Parashara. It is believed that Pulastya imparted spiritual teachings and knowledge to Bhishma, an important figure in the Hindu epic, the Mahabharata.

The main deity of this nakshatra is Chandra, the Moon god. If we were to call this deity the prince charming of the cosmic world, we wouldn't be wrong. He was handsome, he swept people off their feet, he made the ladies swoon and the girls sigh. His drop-dead gorgeous looks made men and gods envious. He was everyone's favourite, though he did get into lots of trouble and earned the anger of the other gods.

Ruling over the lunar cycles, Chandra holds a revered place in Vedic astrology. He was the son of Rishi Atri (one of the Saptarishis) and Anusuya Devi. The Srimad Bhagavatam narrates the story of Chandra's birth. Rishi Atri was concerned about the welfare of the world and hoped for someone who could maintain the balance in the world. He undertook severe penance, and pleased with his austerities, the Trinity blessed him with three sons. They were Chandra, Durvasa, a revered rishi, and Dattatreya, the sage who was worshipped as a god.

One of Chandra's biggest claims to fame is that Shiva wears the crescent moon on his head. This image of Shiva with the moon is known as Chandrashekhar, meaning 'the one who wears the moon on his crown.' How did this happen? Once the gods and the demons were engaged in a fierce battle, they constantly fought for one thing or the other. At Vishnu's suggestion, they joined forces to churn the ocean of milk (Ksheera Sagar) to get amrita, the nectar of immortality. This event was called Samudra Manthan.

Vishnu knew that the devas would not be able to churn the ocean by themselves, they needed the assistance of the asuras. Vishnu's plan was that this nectar would not only give back to the devas the powers they frequently lost to the asuras, but it would also make them immortal. The churning started with the gods on one side and the demons on the other side. All the props were in place. Kurma, the tortoise avatar of Vishnu, was summoned. He plunged into the depths of the ocean. On him was placed Mount Mandara, this was the churning pole. Serpent King Vasuki lent his might as the churning rope. He coiled himself around Mount Mandara. The gods held one end of Vasuki, the demons the other. The churning started and from the depths of the ocean emerged 'halahala', the poison that started enveloping the entire universe with its toxic fumes. Darkness spread its tentacles over the area where the churning of the ocean was happening. Everyone was coughing, choking, and gasping as the fumes were too toxic for them.

The sight frightened both the gods and the demons. They approached Shiva for help. To save them and humankind from the poison, Shiva swallowed it. As the 'halahala' slid into his mouth, Parvati stopped the flow of the poison by capturing it in his throat, so it didn't spread to the rest of

Shiva's body. The poison turned Shiva's neck blue, earning him the name Neelakantha, meaning 'the blue-throated one.' Even though the poison was restricted to Shiva's throat, it started giving him fever. As Chandra is considered to have a cooling effect, the alarmed gods requested him to sit on Shiva's head so that his body temperature would be reduced. Chandra happily obliged. Who would let go of a chance to be of some use to the mighty Mahadeva (another one of Shiva's names)? Chandra did the needful and Shiva's body temperature reduced.

Though the above incident was a blessing for Chandra, he has also received plenty of curses. One from his

The devas and asuras continued churning the ocean until the magical pot of amrita emerged. Both groups wanted the nectar for themselves. For twelve days they fought for this pot of nectar, and the struggle resulted in four drops of nectar falling at four places: Prayagraj, Haridwar, Ujjain, and Nashik. The waters at these locations became sanctified and spiritually rejuvenating. Therefore, once in every twelve years, the Kumbh Mela is held at one of these places, where millions of people take a dip in the rivers flowing in these sacred places, praying for salvation.

father-in-law, Prajapati Daksha, is frequently mentioned. Chandra married twenty-seven of Daksha's daughters; the condition was that he would treat all of them equally. But he failed to honour his promise. Chandra was extremely fond of Rohini and favoured her. Chandra's lack of love made his other wives lose their shine; they started looking dull. When they complained to their father, an angry Prajapati Daksha confronted Chandra. As the miffed Chandra started to leave his father-in-law's palace, deserting his wives in their parental home, Daksha cursed him. The way he had abandoned Daksha's daughters, Chandra too will suffer when his body, his shape, his beauty and radiance leave him.

As Chandra's light and beauty began to fade, things got out of hand as he was also the god of vegetation. The plant life he governed started to die, resulting in the death of the birds, insects, and animals who depended on it.

A worried Chandra requested Brahma for a solution. Brahma asked him to seek Shiva's help. A curse once uttered cannot be taken back, it can just be altered, so that its damage is minimized. Shiva amended the curse by saying that Chandra would get his shape back slowly before he would start waning again, and this cycle of waxing and waning would continue for eternity. During Krishnapaksha (the darkest part of the lunar fortnight), Chandra would wane, and during Shuklapaksha (the brightest part of the lunar fortnight), he would wax. Chandra was satisfied with this solution as there would be days his beauty and power would be visible to the entire world.

A stotram of Chandra deva, perfectly encapsulates his essence:

Dathishagna tushaaraabham ksheeraarnava samudbhavam |
Namaami shashinam somam shambhor-makuta bhooshanam ||

Meaning: I bow to the Moon, whose colour resembles the colour of curd, who shines like ice and snow. I bow to the Moon who has arisen from the ocean of milk and is the ornament on Lord Shiva's head.

The different phases of the moon are called lunar phases. Besides helping farmers ascertain when to plant the seeds or harvest their crops, they also influence people's feelings and actions. The full moon is supposed to affect the mind of the people. It could drive them towards lunacy. Did you know that the word 'lunatic' is a derivative of the Latin word *Luna*, which means Moon?

POPULAR BELIEFS

People born under this nakshatra are known for their curiosity, as though their life is one long search for something or the other. They also have a quick understanding of things – explain something to them once, like a complex chemical equation or a difficult math problem, and they have grasped it in a jiffy. This ability is sure an asset. Perhaps this ability is a blessing from the moon, as it is associated with the subconscious mind, and the power of the subconscious mind is immense and can be harnessed for many different purposes.

An unearthed facet of Chandra deva is that artists of all kinds, especially poets, sought his blessing before they embarked on their creative pursuits, hoping that the moon's radiance and wisdom would give wings to their creativity.

6

ARDRA NAKSHATRA

Deity: Rudra, *The Fierce Incarnation of Shiva*

The word *ardra* in Sanskrit means 'wet,' 'moist,' or 'fresh.' Ardra nakshatra, the sixth nakshatra in Vedic astrology, is associated with qualities like moisture, freshness, and greenness. Moisture is associated with clouds that bring rain. Rain nourishes the earth, the trees, and other vegetation, signifying renewal – especially in nature.

However, moisture need not always be rain, it can also be tears. That gives this nakshatra its symbol – a tear drop. Tear drops symbolize emotional release. Diamond, a gem that withstands immense heat and pressure before emerging as a precious stone, is another symbol of this nakshatra.

Ardra's star is a red giant, one of the brightest stars adorning the night sky, called Betelgeuse or Alpha Orionis that lies in the Orion constellation. This star held an exalted state of reverence in ancient cultures. It was considered important as well as credited with exercising immense influence over earth. Red is also a sign of fierceness, fury, and rage. So, it is really no wonder that the ancient seers considered this star as being the abode of Rudra, the fierce form of Shiva.

Rahu (North Lunar Node) is the planet ruling this nakshatra. He is personified as a deity but is actually one part of the immortal Svarbhanu, an asura who had secretly partaken the nectar of immortality after the Samudra Manthan by disguising himself as a deva and standing amidst them. By the time his deceit came to light, a few drops of nectar had gone down his throat, making him immortal. So, when Vishnu beheaded him with his Sudarshan Chakra, the asura didn't die. His head became known as Rahu and the lower half became Ketu.

The rishi associated with this nakshatra is Pulaha. He, along with many other rishis, was given the crucial responsibility of propagating life on earth and maintaining dharma in the universe.

Rudra, the fierce form of Shiva, is the presiding deity of this nakshatra. The word *rudra* has several meanings: 'ruddy red,' 'fierce,' 'howler,' and 'transformer.' Vedic texts gave Rudra the status of a storm god. He is depicted as the harbinger of commotion, confusion, chaos, and upheaval. Often, this destructive aspect is also considered a precursor of transformation. Change is the essence of Ardra and its deity revels in it.

If you read the story about the birth of Rudra, you will understand why he is called the fierce one as well as the

howler. After Brahma created the universe, he needed people to live in it, to populate it. And not just people, he needed all living beings; he also needed the different species. So, he created four beings, the Kumaras or the four child sages, hoping that they would populate the universe. But these four beings – Sanaka, Sanatkumara, Sanatana, and Sanandana – had no such inclination. All they wanted to do was focus their attention on spiritual pursuits.

Though he grudgingly admitted to himself that they had a valid reason for refusing his order, Brahma was furious that his first four children were going against his wishes. Rage gathered at his forehead, between his eyebrows. His eyes started smouldering. His anger would have consumed the three worlds (heaven, earth, and hell), so fierce it was. The rage intensified so much that Brahma knew his four sons would completely burn under its intensity. So, he did the next best thing he could. He directed the anger from his head in such a way that it was expelled out without harming them or anyone else. From this energy emerged a child, a dark purple infant, wailing and crying furiously. From Brahma's anger was born Rudra.

The moment the child was born, he demanded to know his identity, who he was. Brahma declared that the child's name was Rudra, the wailer and the howler.

The child appeared as half-male and half-female. Brahma ordered it to split into two: a male and a female. Thus, Rudra and his wife, Rudrani, came into existence. Brahma ordered them to split again. Rudra and Rudrani obeyed the creator and once again each split into eleven forms of themselves, producing eleven Rudras and their consorts.

These fierce and howling creatures further populated the world by creating thousands of beings. But these beings were no ordinary people; they were fierce, howling in rage. They were creatures of fire and storm, and destruction followed them everywhere.

Brahma was alarmed. This wasn't part of his plan. These offsprings of Rudra and Rudrani would end up destroying the universe he had so lovingly created.

The eleven pairs of Rudras and Rudranis were just creating without a limit, and this was causing an imbalance in the universe. Brahma requested them to stop producing inauspicious beings and meditate on god. This way they would become calm and cool down. The meditation would remove all the rage, anger, and fury from them and would transform them into auspicious beings.

At this new command, the eleven Rudras and Rudranis all merged into a single male and a single female and started meditating. As they immersed themselves in prayers, they shed their anger and fury and became auspicious. Brahma bestowed on them the names of Shiva, the auspicious one, and Parvati, the one who has risen higher.

There is a poignant story that beautifully highlights another facet of Shiva: if Shiva can manifest Rudra, his fierce form, to fulfil some purpose, he can also suppress or destroy it to fulfil another purpose. Once on a purnima, a full moon night, Krishna was engaged in a Rasa Leela with the gopis of Vrindavan. The beauty of the Rasa Leela attracted Shiva, and he came to the spot to take part in it. Vrinda, the goddess of Vrindavan, stopped him at the edge of the forest, telling him that he wasn't allowed to enter as the only man who could enter the Rasa was Krishna. Her second reason was that Shiva's male ego was preventing his entry and participation in the Rasa.

The Rasa was driving Shiva crazy – the sounds, the music, the colourful clothes, and the dance were all beckoning him. He told Vrinda that as he was Rudra, he had the power to destroy everything, even his ego, which was preventing his entry and participation in the Rasa Leela.

While Vrinda watched, Shiva immediately sat down in the forest and started meditating on Radha, who was at the centre of the Rasa. Radha was the epitome of devotion, and she symbolized pure devotion and supreme love for Krishna. Radha became aware of Shiva's meditation and as she couldn't leave the dance, she sent her friend Lalita to go and help Shiva. Lalita arrived at the place Shiva was meditating. She was enchanted with Shiva's yogi form, deeply absorbed in meditation.

Lalita taught Shiva how to develop the ego of a female goddess so that he could take part in the Rasa. Shiva absorbed all the knowledge like a sincere student, but his body still remained that of a male's. Lalita then accompanied Shiva to the banks of River Yamuna. Heeding her instructions, Shiva took a dip in the waters. When Shiva emerged, he had shed the male body and taken the form of a gopi. He could now enter the Rasa Leela. The omniscient Krishna was aware of this gopi's true identity. Seeing the new gopi, Krishna was delighted and became mischievous. As Shiva is also called Maheshwara and he had assumed the form of a gopi, Krishna named him Gopeshwara.

Pilgrims thronging Vrindavan invoke Shiva in the form of Gopeshwara seeking inner transformation. Just as Rudra shed his masculine ego to enter the Rasa as a gopi, he would do the same with them – destroy their ego, making them fit to receive Krishna's grace.

POPULAR BELIEFS

People born under this nakshatra are observant. One look at any person or an object, and they have memorized every little detail about them, just like Rudra can sum up any situation with a single glance. They are also sensitive and can be hurt easily. But in spite of this aspect of their nature, they are toughies when it comes to facing difficult situations.

Though Rudra is considered destructive, he brings about a change or transformation, one that leads to a renewal, a change for the better.

7

PUNARVASU NAKSHATRA

Deity: Aditi, *Mother of the Universe*

Punarvasu, the seventh nakshatra, occupies a very lucky slot: number seven. The name is derived from the Sanskrit words *punar*, meaning 'again,' 'repeat,' or 'repetition,' and *vasu*, which means 'a ray of light' or 'goodness.' Hence, Punarvasu means 'good again' or 'wealthy again.'

Castor and Pollux, the two bright stars of Punarvasu, are located in the Gemini constellation. They can be seen easily in the night sky. Castor is also known as Alpha Geminorum and Pollux as Beta Geminorum. Pollux is brighter of the two.

In many ancient cultures, these two bright stars were considered twins. In Greek and Roman mythology, they are twin brothers, referred to as Dioscuri. They symbolized an unbreakable bond and were entrusted with the responsibility of rescuing people who were stranded at sea or were facing danger in a war.

The symbol of this nakshatra is a quiver full of arrows. Sometimes the symbol could also be a single arrow. Whether a quiver full or single, the arrow remains constant. Arrows were divine weapons used by gods, ancient kings, and warriors. These arrows contained a lot of power that could be invoked using mantras. Some arrows returned to the archers after finding their marks, some arrows empowered with mantras could only be used once, and some arrows were enhanced with different powers.

The ruling planet of Punarvasu nakshatra is Jupiter (Brihaspati). It is the largest planet in the solar system, a giant mass of gas, with a diameter that is over eleven times that of Earth. It was named after Jupiter, the king of the gods in Roman mythology.

Kratu is the rishi associated with this nakshatra. It is believed that Kratu was present when Arjuna's birth celebration was being held. He was also a part of Indra's council. Both events show how revered and important this rishi was.

The deity of this nakshatra is Aditi, the mother goddess. Her name means 'unfettered,' 'unbound,' and 'boundless.' This goddess of abundance is considered the mother of all divine beings in the universe.

Known as Devamata, mother of the devas, Aditi kept a low-profile, preferring to let her work speak for itself. She was content with bringing up her children and looking after her husband and his hermitage. As the universal mother, she protected and guarded all forms of life. Some even credit her with creation, believing that the universe was inside her womb before creation took place.

Symbolic of the boundless heaven, Aditi personifies the sky and sustains the entire universe. Her vahana is a rooster, a symbol of strength and valour. She is depicted with ten hands, holding a trishul in one hand, a sword in another, and one of her hands in the protective abhaya mudra. This goddess slays demons and protects her devotees from the difficulties they encounter and also bestows on them optimism, peace, and strength.

Aditi was Prajapati Daksha's daughter. She lived with her husband, Rishi Kashyapa, in his hermitage. Her helpful nature and devotion pleased the rishi, and he offered to grant her a boon. She requested for a powerful and ideal son. This son was none other than Indra. Aditi is also the mother of the twelve Adityas, the solar deities.

The names of the twelve Adityas vary in the different Puranas. It is believed that the twelve Adityas represent the twelve aspects of the sun and also signify the twelve months in the calendar.

According to the Vishnu Purana, the twelve Adityas are:

1. Amsa
2. Aryaman
3. Bhaga
4. Dhuti
5. Mitra
6. Pushan
7. Sakra
8. Savitr
9. Tvastr
10. Varuna
11. Visnu
12. Vivasat

Aditi's sister Diti was also married to Rishi Kashyapa. On seeing her co-wife have children, Diti was overcome with grief and jealousy. She asked her husband, Kashyapa, to beget a son for her too. This made Aditi scared and insecure as she didn't want Diti's child to be superior to her son. So, when Diti became pregnant with her first child, who was destined to be *daitya* (an asura), Aditi incited

Indra to harm them. A furious Diti then cursed her sister that Aditi's child would keep losing his kingdom, power, and prestige to Diti's children and that Aditi would also lose her children.

Diti became the mother of daityas who were forever at war with the devas. They opposed the divine cosmic order or dharma. The asuras often defeated the gods, resulting in their head, Indra, losing his kingdom many times.

When Aditi was reborn as Devaki, the second part of the curse was fulfilled. Devaki lost seven of her children due to her cruel brother Kamsa. A prophecy that Devaki's eighth son would result in his death made Kamsa kill his sister's

Going by Aditi's stature in the pantheon of gods, there should have been many temples dedicated to her. But sadly, that's not the case. There were just a couple of temples that hosted sculptures of this mother goddess, but now these idols have made their way into museums, to be preserved for posterity. The stone statue of Aditi that adorned the Sangameshwara Temple is now housed in the Alampur Site Museum, Telangana. Likewise, the statue earlier found in the Naganatha Temple now stands in the Archaeological Museum Badami, Karnataka.

children to prevent it from coming true. But curses have a strange way of materializing.

According to the Mahabharata, Aditi was cursed by Sage Budha, too. One day, Sage Budha (known as Mercury) visited Aditi's house asking for food. As Aditi was feeding her children at that time, she asked him to wait. This made the sage angry and he cursed Aditi that she would take birth again and again.

POPULAR BELIEFS

People born under this nakshatra are known for their patience and quiet nature, a lot like the mother goddess Aditi. Though they are generous, again a trait derived from Aditi, they also like their generosity to be rewarded (this is where they differ from Aditi, as she expects nothing in return). Just like when you do someone a favour you want them to help you back, as a mark of gratitude. They believe in the adage that their good turn deserves another one in return.

Aditi makes us realize that one need not be high profile to have a whole lot of important responsibilities (of giving birth to the gods and raising them) thrust on their shoulders. Some people do their work silently without drawing attention either to themselves or their work.

8

PUSHYA NAKSHATRA

Deity: Brihaspati, *The Guru of All Gods*

The eighth nakshatra, Pushya means 'nourisher,' 'nurturer,' and 'yielding.' All these translations carry in their wombs the very essence of this nakshatra. Pushya was earlier known as Tishya, meaning 'auspicious.' It has another name – Sidhya, which translates to 'prosperous.' All these names point to the kind nature of this nakshatra. Some feel that Pushya could also mean a flower. A flower is one of the most beautiful and gentlest creations of God. Flowers have such a short lifespan but they end up making anyone who sees them happy.

Pushya nakshatra is represented by three stars: Theta Cancri, Gamma Cancri (Asellus Borealis), and Eta Cancri. These stars lie in the constellation of Cancer. None of them are bright, and are barely visible to the naked eye in dark skies.

The symbol of this nakshatra is the udder of a cow, a reflection of being the nourishing and nurturing one. In ancient Vedic times, a cow was one of the most revered animals. Even today, cows are highly venerated and considered holy. Other symbols of this nakshatra are a circle, a lotus, and a wheel. Wheel represents movement and progress. It is also symbolic of the cyclical nature of time and karma, connecting it with the ruling planet of this nakshatra – Saturn (Shani).

The planetary ruler of this nakshatra, Saturn is the second-largest planet in the solar system. It has rings around it that are composed of ice particles, dust, and rocky debris.

Marichi is the rishi associated with this nakshatra. Marichi and his wife, Kala, had a son whose fame spread far and wide. This son was none other than Rishi Kashyapa, who is considered a Prajapati by many. Rishi Kashyapa furthered the creation along with his wives, and is considered the father of many beings, including devas, asuras, nagas, and all of humanity.

The deity of this nakshatra, Brihaspati (planet Jupiter), is a powerhouse of skills. Imagine your favourite teacher, the one you are in awe of, the one who has answers to all your curious questions, the one who is highly knowledgeable and intellectual. When Brihaspati spoke, everyone listened attentively so as not to miss a single word that came from his mouth. He was the priest of the gods, the chief advisor of the gods, as well the guru of the devas, the lord of mantras, and other rituals like yagna and initiations.

Brihaspati was the son of Rishi Angiras and his wife Surupa. Angiras, Brahma's son, was believed to be one of the first fire deities and a guru of divine wisdom, and Surupa's devotion and faith were unmatched in the cosmic world. Brihaspati inherited both his parents' virtues and character. Right from childhood, he displayed a religious nature, visiting sacred places to pray to the gods. The young boy's devotion and dedication pleased Shiva. He appointed Brihaspati as a guru of all the gods and granted him the status of the chief priest of heaven. If these two positions weren't enough, Shiva entrusted to Brihaspati the custody of the planet Jupiter. It must be lovely to be the custodian of a planet. The current billionaires own islands, while the powerful rishis of yore ruled over planets. Just imagine whenever Brihaspati wanted some peace and solitude, he could just zoom off to his private planet.

Now, with so much power and responsibilities thrust on his capable shoulders, Brihaspati had made himself so indispensable that the gods were lost without him. He was their priest and their chief advisor. So, he never zipped off to his private planet as he was always needed for something or the other.

It is but natural that with great power comes a huge ego. Indra, a *shishya* (student) of Brihaspati, is a prime example of that. In the Srimad Bhagavatam there is a story about how Indra was taught a lesson by his guru Brihaspati. A guru will never tolerate an egoistic disciple and will teach him a lesson. The same happened with Indra. One day, Indra was reclining on his royal throne in the large and grand hall of his palace, enjoying all the luxuries of the cosmic world. Beside him sat his wife and around them were his assembly of ministers and demigods.

At that moment Brihaspati entered the assembly hall. Ideally when the guru enters a room, the disciples stop whatever they were doing and rush to prostrate to the guru and welcome him. But Indra was lost in his own world of splendour that he didn't bother to greet or welcome the divine priest. The king of heaven had completely forgotten both the duties of a host and a shishya.

Though Brihaspati was furious that he had been overlooked for some silly entertainment, he didn't utter a curse or rebuke Indra. He quietly left the palace. To show

Indra his place, Brihaspati, with his yogic powers, made himself invisible. This was Brihaspati's way of showing Indra that he and the devas were nothing without their guru.

Suddenly Indra realized that he had insulted his guru by not paying his respects to him. Indra ran out of the hall, hoping to catch up with his guru and beg his forgiveness. But Brihaspati was nowhere to be seen. Indra searched and searched but he couldn't find his guru.

Without their powerful guru, Indra and the other gods were bereft of the protective shield and armour his presence in their lives provided. They were scared and vulnerable and were susceptible to attacks. Without a priest and a guru, they couldn't conduct any rituals. A guru's presence was crucial to the rituals and yagnas.

This was the chance the asuras were waiting for. They stormed heaven, attacked and defeated the gods easily. Indra learnt an important lesson, that to ignore one's guru can be catastrophic. In this case, he lost his kingdom.

Indra, as usual, got scared and rushed to Brahma to help him out of this problem. Brahma's advice was to get another priest in Brihaspati's place. He suggested that Indra request Mayasura's (the architect of the asuras) son Visvarupa, a three-headed creature, to become the priest of the gods. Visvarupa wasn't in favour of this position, actually he had no interest in it. But as he couldn't say an outright no to the king of gods, he reluctantly agreed.

The first thing Visvarupa did in his official capacity as the priest of the gods was to teach Indra how to arm himself with the protection of the Narayana Kavacha. This was no invisibility cloak, but a mystical and magical coat of armour made from mantras that gave the coat its power. And all these mantras were dedicated to Vishnu. With this powerful shield, Indra effortlessly threw the asuras from his kingdom.

Now, herein lies the catch. Visvarupa was a sly and a wily creature. Every time he performed a ritual for Indra, he secretly hid a portion of the offerings to give to his asura relatives, so that they too derived the power and the benefit of the heavenly ritual. The asuras were delighted with this secret stash that was empowering them with no effort from their side. The devas had no idea that they were losing out on getting the full benefit of the yagnas.

One day Indra became aware of this deceit. In anger, he chopped off the three heads of Visvarupa. When Mayasura heard about this, he became furious and his rage ended up creating a terrifying monster called Vrtra. This monster was giant and immensely powerful. When Vrtra entered heaven, all the gods unleashed an array of weapons at him. Vrtra was like an ancient Godzilla. Opening his gigantic mouth, he started swallowing the weapons one by one, as though they were something sweet and chocolatey. The gods were alarmed. At this rate all their weapons would be inside Vrtra's stomach and could never be retrieved.

They rushed to Vishnu for help. Vishnu explained to the gods that the special armour that Visvarupa had created for Indra was a technique he had learnt from his father Mayasura. Mayasura had acquired this knowledge from the smart Ashvini Kumaras.

Vishnu advised the gods to appeal to Dadhichi for help as he had the secret knowledge of this special and magical armour, which had made his body and bones powerful. Vishnu asked them to request Dadhichi to give his bones so that a weapon could be made. When Indra requested Dadhichi, the kind-hearted sage was happy to give up his body, through his powers, so that his bones could be used for the noble cause of defeating Vrtra. As per Vishnu's instructions, Vishwakarma made a thunderbolt for Indra from Dadhichi's bones. Armed with this powerful weapon, Indra attacked Vrtra and killed him. Peace once again settled over heaven.

But this peace came with a high price. Indra was afflicted with guilt for having killed a brahmin. To repent for this sin, he retreated to Lake Mansarovar and hid inside a stem of a lotus to perform penance. Later, Brihaspati came to Mansarovar and requested Indra to return to his position as the king of gods.

POPULAR BELIEFS

People born under this nakshatra are compassionate and nurturing. They are generous and very protective of their loved ones, just like the guru Brihaspati who selflessly shared his immense knowledge with his shishyas and protected them from the asuras. They also have a strong sense of purpose, of wanting to achieve their goals.

The story of Brihaspati teaching Indra a lesson shows the power of a guru and the consequences of not respecting one's teacher. If the guru is displeased, then things can go drastically wrong for the disciple. So, honouring one's guru is key to spiritual growth and lasting success.

9

ASHLESHA NAKSHATRA

Deity: Nagas, *The Eternal Snake*

Ashlesha nakshatra takes the number nine position. Nine is considered lucky by many. But when one hears the translation of the name Ashlesha – 'coiling,' 'clinging,' 'entwining' – it conjures up images of creatures most people fear. Snakes. Serpents. It is for this reason Ashlesha is called the Clinging Star, referring to its snake-like imagery and association. Even the name Naga is associated with it. Ashlesha may also be a derivative of the word *Shesha*, the serpent king or the snake god.

This nakshatra boasts of a collection of stars known in modern astronomy as Epsilon Hydrae, Zeta Hydrae, Delta Hydrae, Mu Hydrae, Rho Hydrae, and Sigma Hydrae (Minchir). They are located in the constellation Hydra, the largest constellation in the sky. Hydra is also known as the Water Snake in Greek mythology, making it easy to guess the main symbol of this nakshatra – a coiled snake or serpent. Serpents have a connection with two gods from the trinity. The snake Vasuki is coiled around Shiva's neck, and Vishnu reclines on Sheshnaga.

Mercury (Budha) is the ruling planet of this nakshatra. This smallest planet in the solar system has been named after the ancient Roman god Mercurius, who was the messenger of the gods and the god of commerce and communication. Vashishta is the rishi associated with this nakshatra. This rishi's two cows, the wish-fulfilling cow Kamadhenu and her offspring Nandini, were coveted by many and also caused a fight between Vashishta and Vishwamitra.

Serpents are secretive and cunning, with a tendency to deceive and even hypnotize people. Remember the *ichchadhari* snakes popular in Indian folklore, who could shape-shift and assume any form? Poison is their weapon to annihilate their prey. On the flip side, they are considered semi-divine creatures and worshipped. They are also said to possess insight and intuition. Though serpents are always buried under shrouds of mystery and considered an enigma, they are said to be crucial to maintain the balance in the universe.

You may have heard about the nagas. Nagas that comprises the entire serpent kingdom of the celestial world are the deity of this nakshatra. Depicted as half-human and half-serpent, these creatures are famed for their strength, power, knowledge, and wisdom. In Hindu tradition, there are fourteen *lokas* (realms) – seven higher and seven lower – and serpents can be found in all. They didn't leave heaven, earth, or water (lakes, seas, and oceans) alone. They are everywhere.

It is believed in various religious traditions that the nagas and serpents live in the netherworld, called Patala loka. This realm lies below the earth and is further divided into seven realms: Atala, Vitala, Sutala, Talatala, Mahatala, Rasatala, and Patala, with the seventh one belonging to the nagas. It is also called Naga loka.

These nagas have a showstopper. It is none other than the giant, thousand-headed serpent Sheshnaga, also known as Shesha or Adishesha. With a crown adorned on each head, this superstar of the snake world serves as Vishnu's

divine couch. He is considered a symbol of infinity and timelessness, and is worshipped by millions. The young snakes must have grown up hearing stories about Sheshnaga from their parents.

Despite all the fame and popularity, Sheshnaga remains humble and devoted. In the Puranas, he is entrusted with a lot of responsibilities: he holds all the planets and the earth on his many hoods and maintains the cosmic balance. Sheshnaga is usually depicted as floating in the ocean of milk called Ksheera Sagar, his large body coiled in layers, with Vishnu resting on him and Lakshmi seated by his side.

Why is Shesha such a revered snake? The answer to this mystery lies in the Sanskrit meaning of Shesha's name, which translates to 'he who remains.' This has two symbolisms. First is the fact that Shesha is constantly by Vishnu's side. Second, Shesha is believed to remain intact even when the world is destroyed at the end of each kalpa (cycle). He existed before the universe was created and he will continue to live after the universe is destroyed.

In the Mahabharata, there is a story about the birth of Sheshnaga. Rishi Kashyapa, the son of Rishi Marichi, married seventeen daughters of Prajapati Daksha. (Daksha had so many daughters that he was the father-in-law of half the celestial world.) Of all his wives, Kashyapa loved Kadru the most. So happy was he with her that one day, feeling ecstatic, he gave her a boon. She could ask for anything. Can you guess what she asked for?

Well, Kadru requested for a thousand sons. Kashyapa granted her this strange wish. Within a few days, she birthed a thousand eggs. Though her situation and the eggs puzzled her, she placed them in a warm spot so they would hatch.

As the days passed, the eggs hatched into a thousand snakes. The eldest of these was Sheshnaga. He was kind and noble and he disliked harming anyone, unlike his siblings who revelled in their cruelty. When their behaviour went beyond his tolerance, he fled to different places to escape his siblings and meditate in peace. Lack of food and water coupled with his intense *tapasya* (penance) made his body shrink. But he continued his austerities, pleasing Brahma, who appeared before him to grant him a boon. Just like you have to work hard and be sincere in order to please your parents so they can grant you a wish!

Instead of asking for powers and other things, Sheshnaga requested that he be granted self-control so he could continue his austerities without interruption. Pleased with this humble request, Brahma bestowed upon him the blessing of self-control, advising him to continue his tapasya under the earth to make it stable. This is the reason Sheshnaga lives in Patala loka.

It is said that every time Vishnu incarnated on earth, his serpent Sheshnaga incarnated alongside him. When Vishnu took the avatar of Lord Rama in the Treta Yuga, Sheshnaga incarnated as Lakshmana, who didn't leave his brother's side even during his fourteen-year-long exile. When Vishnu assumed the form of Krishna in the Dvapara Yuga, Sheshnaga preceded him as his brother Balarama. Even in the Satya Yuga, when Vishnu incarnated as Narasimha to vanquish the demon Hiranyakashipu, Sheshnaga incarnated as a seat for Vishnu. This time the snake was in his original form. In each avatar, he served Vishnu with complete devotion.

In the Hindu epics, Sheshnaga, along with Kurma the tortoise, holds the earth and stabilizes it. As this gigantic snake with several coils moves forward by uncoiling his body, time too moves forward. It was believed that when Sheshnaga yawned, earthquakes happened.

POPULAR BELIEFS

People born under this nakshatra are thoughtful and cautious when meeting others, carefully observing before they open up, just like a snake is always wary of other creatures. They have a keen sense of strategy and enjoy stimulating mental challenges. They also have a sharp wit, are responsible and efficient, and possess a desire for knowledge.

Sheshnaga's life makes one realize that one can rise above one's destiny through determination and self-effort, just like this revered snake shrugged off the garb of his ferocious species to become a sacred snake, close to the preserver of the universe, and revered by humankind through the ages.

10

MAGHA NAKSHATRA

Deity: Pitrs, *Honourable Ancestors*

Magha, the tenth nakshatra, is considered to be the brightest and the largest nakshatra. *Magha* translates to 'mighty,' 'magnificent,' 'great,' 'bountiful,' and 'beneficent.' All these words immediately evoke a sense of royalty, a majestic, larger-than-life image, which is represented in the symbol of this nakshatra – a throne, or, to be more precise, 'a royal chamber with a throne inside it.' One glimpse of a throne and people associate it with power and prestige, all things royal and regal.

A sickle-shaped group of stars adorning the night sky represents this nakshatra. The principal star of this nakshatra is Regulus (Alpha Leonis). *Regulus* is Latin for 'little king.' The brightest star in the constellation Leo (Latin for 'lion'), it is also called *Cor Leonis*, the lion's heart. The star Regulus held great importance in ancient cultures and was often considered the celestial seat of power.

Its companion stars that form the sickle are Al Jabhah (Eta Leonis), Algieba (Gamma Leonis), Adhafera (Zeta Leonis), Rasalas (Mu Leonis), Algenubi (Epsilon Leonis). While in Vedic astrology the nakshatra is symbolized by a royal throne, many cultures see this cluster resembling a lion.

The ruling planet of this nakshatra is Ketu (South Lunar Node). It is believed that Ketu is responsible for the lunar eclipse and is representative of enlightenment, spirituality, liberation, as well as detachment.

Angiras is the rishi associated with this nakshatra. He taught Brahmavidya – the knowledge of Brahman, the absolute ultimate reality – to worthy spiritual seekers. Brahmavidya is considered the path to spiritual enlightenment.

The ruling deities of this nakshatra are the ancestors, known as 'pitrs' or 'pitris.' It is believed that the pitrs look after their descendants living on the physical plane, guiding and blessing them like guardian angels. Think of all the times your family elders held the 'shraddha ceremony' for the departed ancestors. Through this ceremony, the descendants pay their respects to them, thanking them for their guidance and blessings and also honouring their lives on earth and keeping their memories ever fresh in the family members' minds. This practice has been a part of Hindu culture since time immemorial and is a sacred way of maintaining our connection with our roots.

According to the puranas, after leaving the physical world, the souls of our ancestors dwell in the Pitra loka, which is the world of ancestors. This is like a transit room where the recently departed souls meet their ancestors before continuing their journey, either to higher realms or returning to earth in another form, based on their karma. Most ancient cultures mention such a world of ancestors.

How did the pitrs make their way into the universe? Let's explore that story. Brahma was looking at the water around him. There was silence all around. Creation of the universe was yet to start. Even the air was still, as though awaiting the creator's instructions. Brahma sat still and created the seven pitrs. Four of the pitrs had forms, while three were made of light. Brahma was enchanted with all seven. They looked lovely, even the ones with forms glowed as bright as the ones without forms. He blessed them that their food would be the *shraddha* (funeral offerings to the deceased souls) and *tarpanas* (peace offerings to the devas, rishis, and the pitrs). In a yagna or a homa the gods are invoked in the fire, but in shraddhas and tarpanas, the pitrs are invoked in water held in palms cupped together.

Let's learn a hymn honouring the pitrs:

O the superiors of the twice-born ones! The group of Pitṛs, the Agniṣvāttas and Varhiṣads, arose from those drops of perspiration which fell from his (Brahmā) body. *Kalika Puran 2.46*

Pitrs can be devah pitarah, the divine pitrs who live in heavenly abodes and were accorded a godly status, and the manusyah pitrs, the deceased humans who dwell in the netherworlds and sometimes also in heavenly abodes. Even the souls of our deceased ancestors become pitrs.

The best thing about the pitrs is that they are eternal and never cease to exist, and at the end of each mahayuga they are reborn so that the world is revived and new creation rises from them.

There is an interesting story about the pitrs. Jaratkaru was an ascetic of the highest order, he was also one of the pitrs. He was known for the strict vows he made, like he could just survive on air. No food, no water. One day while he was walking around on earth, he came across his ancestors hanging by a thread from a hole in a tree. The strands of the thread had worn away, only a single one was left. Hungry rats were gnawing the ancestors' bodies. Jaratkaru was alarmed. He rushed towards his ancestors, hoping to save them. The pitrs narrated their sad tale. They were rishis and they had all lost their children. Pointing to the single strand by which they were hanging, they told Jaratkaru that that particular thread was symbolic of him. And as he was an ascetic and had no family or children, that thread too would wear away unless he married and had children who would carry his lineage forward. They begged Jaratkaru to fulfil his duty, urging him that he was morally bound as their last descendant to carry forward their lineage, his son would be their salvation.

Jaratkaru's heart melted at his ancestors' plight. He promised them that he would marry but only if he found a woman who had the same name as his. No one knew why he wanted a namesake wife and didn't demand too much of his time, which he wanted to utilize for spiritual pursuits and austerities. As an ascetic, he couldn't afford a demanding wife. Time passed, and in spite of his search, he didn't come across any woman who was his namesake. He was saddened that he couldn't save his ancestors.

Alarmed that the thread was wearing away, they suggested that he make this announcement loudly and ask for the maiden as alms. This guidance proved successful as

Vasuki, the king of snakes, heard the announcement and brought his sister to Jaratkaru. She was named Jaratkaru as well, just as he wanted. Jaratkaru married Vasuki's sister and they lived happily until one day the wife woke Jaratkaru so that he could perform his prayers. Jaratkaru felt insulted by this action of his wife, of reminding him about his prayers that were always on his mind, and he left her. But before leaving her, he told her that the child she was carrying in her womb would become a powerful sage. Perhaps this prophecy and blessing was his way of easing his guilt about abandoning his wife. Vasuki's sister was saddened that her husband had left her. She found consolation in the prophecy that her child would make a mark in the world of sages. Sometime later, she gave birth to a son named Astika. When Astika grew older, he saved the snakes from a snake sacrifice and became a saviour of the snakes.

Though pitrs, could directly refer to our ancestors, the ancestors of each family, there is also the macro image where these pitrs are the forefathers of humanity – the Prajapatis. These pitrs, our forefathers, went on to produce powerful creatures who went a step ahead to produce more creatures (both humans and the different species). In short, pitrs are the founding fathers of the world.

The different types of pitrs must take care of the souls of their descendants after they have died and have to move on to their next destination, aka a new birth. In this transition period between two births when their karmas are being checked, a newly deceased person's soul is definitely not peaceful. It becomes the duty of the pitrs to bring peace to the souls and grant them the prosperity of a good birth. The hardworking pitrs do this through prayers and meditation, through sacrifices. The pitrs guide the souls in the afterlife. The afterlife is not easy to navigate; one needs guidance and company there.

The pitrs once they see the newly deceased souls, prepare them by giving them guidance and advise, as the deceased souls will be facing one of fiercest invigilators one will ever encounter. Yama, the god of death, will be judging the souls by their deeds on earth and will be handing out suitable rewards or punishments.

POPULAR BELIEFS

People born under this nakshatra are confident by nature. They are also powerful, influential, and have a tendency to lose their temper easily. They also like to follow ethics and moral rules of conduct; perhaps following in the path of the ancestors of humankind, who went about their work, following all the rules and laws set by the creator. Just like that one child in class who refuses to break a rule or follow the naughty behaviour of other classmates when the teacher's back is turned.

The Pitr loka is a serene place, filled with a divine light, with the inhabitants (pitrs) engaged in meditation and prayers. Even rishis and prajapatis reside in Pitr loka, and they have the responsibility of guarding dharma and ensuring the cosmic order is maintained with their prayers and spiritual practices. The afterlife isn't all about rest and relaxation.

11

PURVA PHALGUNI NAKSHATRA

Deity: Bhaga, *The God on Everyone's Wishlist*

The eleventh nakshatra in the Vedic lunar zodiac is Purva Phalguni. The name means 'former reddish one' or 'former little fig tree.' In many ancient cultures, the fig tree is believed to be a symbol of fertility and abundance.

This nakshatra is represented in the sky by two bright stars known as Delta Leonis and Theta Leonis, located at the back of the Leo constellation.

Delta Leonis is also known as Zosma, and Theta Leonis as Chertan.

The symbols of this nakshatra are front legs of a bed, two poles of a swinging hammock, or fig tree. When our ancient seers looked at this pair of stars, all they could see was the front legs of a cot or a bed or two poles of a swinging hammock. One will never figure out why the sages see all these strange symbols.

The planet Venus (Shukra) rules over this nakshatra. Venus is named after the Roman goddess of love and beauty. The planet is also considered Earth's sister planet as both are similar in size and mass.

Rishi Atri is associated with this nakshatra. This famous rishi was always engaged in prayers, and his tapasyas ensured the Trinity's blessings on him. He was so exalted that the fifth Mandala, or the Rig Veda Book 5, is named after him. It is called the Atri Mandala and has eighty-seven shlokas attributed to Atri and his family.

The deity of this nakshatra is Bhaga. If there was one Vedic god who was on top of everyone's worship wishlist, it would be Bhaga, the god of good fortune and prosperity. *Bhaga* means 'fortune,' 'wealth,' and 'power' in Sanskrit. The son of Aditi and Kashyapa, he is one of the twelve Adityas, a group of solar deities. If you want your good actions to reap rich dividends – not for financial investments, it is the karmic rewards that we are discussing here – then it is Bhaga whose favour you'd want to win.

Bhaga's appearance can take one's breath away and make people sigh. Dawn has just broken. The first sliver of golden light pierces the sky like a sharp arrow that spreads a glow of a shimmery sunshine in the sky. Through that halo of golden light appears a deity with a gigantic body, his bright face radiant with a smile. His entire body is as bright as the sun. Carrying flowers in his hands, standing in his golden chariot driven by golden horses, he announces the arrival of the sun. When he isn't heralding the morning sun, he sits on a big lotus and watches everything with a gentle smile on his face. This god sure has the pleasant looks associated with the god of wealth and luck.

However, for all his good looks, there is a small problem – Bhaga is blind. Let's explore the story that describes how Bhaga lost his sight. When Prajapati Daksha organized a grand yagna, he invited the movers and shakers of the cosmic world, but his son-in-law Shiva and daughter Sati were deliberately excluded. Everyone knew that Daksha disliked Shiva.

Bhaga was not only one of the VIP guests attending the yagna, but also one of the priests presiding at the yagna. It was his duty to ensure that the yagna went off smoothly. Dressed in his best clothes, his jewellery glittering and the gems in them twinkling like stars, Bhaga was constantly by Daksha's side, his bright, watchful eyes scanning the venue to ensure that everything was in order.

At Mount Kailash, Sati had just announced to her husband, Shiva, that she had decided to go to the yagna, even though she wasn't invited. Shiva tried to dissuade her, but Sati was adamant. When she reached there, Sati was hurt to see that a place was reserved for all the gods, even the demigods, but there was no place for her husband. When she approached her father, he insulted her. Feeling humiliated, Sati immolated herself in the yagna fire, shocking the gathering of gods and sages.

When this news reached Shiva, he was furious. His fury created a fierce warrior called Virabhadra. It is said that in anger Shiva threw a lock of his matted hair on the ground and from it appeared Virabhadra. Shiva sent him to the place where the yagna was being conducted. Virabhadra arrived at the yagna site and started destroying everything. Some of the VIP guests engaged in a battle with Virabhadra to stop him. Bhaga was one of the gods who tried to prevent Virabhadra from causing harm. The brave god took on this fierce creature while the other guests watched wide-eyed. Virabhadra defeated Bhaga and in anger blinded him. He caused harm to many other deities, too.

His blindness may be one of the reasons Bhaga distributes wealth unevenly. In the Rig Veda, there are sixty hymns mentioning Bhaga, a divine distributor. Bhaga is also associated with marriage and one's standing in society, aka the social order. Some Rig Vedic hymns attribute material blessings in the form of abundant harvests, cattle, and other possessions – which can all be counted as wealth – to Bhaga. Bhaga bestows spiritual blessings, too, in the form of devotion and faith. He was also tasked with the duty of making marriages successful. He shared this responsibility with Aryaman, who was another Vedic deity.

In the post-Vedic period, Bhaga's importance declined. In fact, the very landscape of our gods changed in that period. Many deities faded into oblivion, paving the path for others to rise to prominence.

Let me teach you all a mantra to please Bhaga. (You never know your parents may increase your pocket money.) It is a simple mantra. Try it!

Om Sree Bhagaya Namaha

Here are some hymns dedicated to Bhaga:

1. *Pratar agnim, Pratar Indram havamahe pratar mitra varuna, prathar aswina,*
Pratar bhagam pooshanam Brahmanaspathim pratha soma muthaa rudram huvema.

Meaning: At dawn we invoke Agni (fire god), at dawn we pray to Indra, at dawn we invoke Mitra (sun god), at dawn we call on Varuna (god of rain) and the two Ashvini Kumaras (the divine doctors)

At dawn we invoke Bhaga (god of fortune and wealth), at dawn we beseech Poosha (god of way and path), at dawn we invoke Brihaspati (teacher of devas), at dawn we call on Soma (moon god) and Rudra (god of anger).

2. *Bhaga parenthar bhaga sathyaradho bhage maam dhiyamudavaa dhadhanaa,*
Bhaga parano janaya gobhir aswai bhaga para nrbhirnravantha sayaama.

Meaning: Oh Bhaga, cross our way (come before us), oh Bhaga bestower of true gifts, continue showering your gifts on us,

Oh Bhaga, add the wealth of cows and horses to our store, oh Bhaga bless us and grant us men and kings.

3. *Uthedanim bhaga vantha sayomotha paripithwa utha madhye ahnam,*
Uthoditha magavana sooryasya vayam devaanaam sumathou sayama.

Meaning: Bestow on us wealth and luck and when light breaks during noon,

And even at the time of sunset, let us experience the good grace of all the gods.

4. *Bhaga eva bhagavanasthu Devaasthena vayam bhagavantha sayama,*
Tham thavaa bhaga sarva ijjohaveethi sa no bhaga purethaa bhaveha.

Meaning: Let Bhaga be the one who showers on me wealth and luck, and oh gods, make us blessed and lucky

Oh Bhaga we beseech you with all our mind, that you Bhaga be our guide here (in this world).

POPULAR BELIEFS

People born under this nakshatra are creative and warm-hearted and have a tendency to blend in rather than stand out, a lot like Bhaga who was never in the limelight, staying in the background, though he was the god of fortune. People born under this nakshatra are friendly and have an affectionate nature. They enjoy spending time in the company of their loved ones, be it family or friends.

Bhaga has disappeared from the pantheon of gods, as his duties have been taken over by Lakshmi now; people pray to her for wealth and prosperity. Even Vishnu absorbed some of Bhaga's duties. Now Bhaga survives in name only, as it looks like the name Bhagya Lakshmi has been a derivative of Bhaga.

12

UTTARA PHALGUNI NAKSHATRA

Deity: Aryaman, *The Brand Ambassador of Hospitality*

Uttara Phalguni means 'latter reddish one' or 'latter fig tree.' As Phalguna month is associated with spring, so is this twelfth nakshatra.

It is represented in the sky by the two stars Beta Leonis, also known as Denebola, and 93 Leonis. The second-brightest star in Leo constellation, Denebola is the tail end of the constellation.

Uttara Phalguni nakshatra not only has a similar-sounding name to Purva Phalguni, the symbols for both the nakshatras are quite close, too. One would assume that the placement of the two stars would be relatively easy for the ancient seers to decipher. But our ancient sages weren't big fans of simple explanations, they loved complexity and liked to give their brain cells a lot of exercise. What they saw was the two rear legs of a bed or cot, that too a funeral cot, and this became the symbol of this nakshatra.

The powerful Sun (Surya) is the ruling planet of Uttara Phalguni. Sun worship forms an important part of our culture as the sun is considered one of the *sakshat* (visible) gods. Makar Sankranti, Pongal, and Chhath Puja are some of the festivals honouring the sun.

Pulastya is the rishi associated with this nakshatra. It is said that through the power of his tapasya and his immense spiritual energy, Pulastya could create large celestial realms and entire worlds with precision and perfection.

This nakshatra's deity is Aryaman, one of the twelve Adityas (solar deities). This early Vedic deity's name means 'partner,' 'close friend,' or 'companion.' He presides over favours, kindness, and patronage. When you want someone to do you a big favour, you can pray to Aryaman. Aryaman's blessings are precious. We can call Aryaman the brand ambassador of hospitality. Remember the famous saying *Athiti devo bhava*? Aryaman was a firm believer that guest is god.

Of the twelve Adityas, Aryaman is the deity everyone wants as their BFF. This upholder of dharma also safeguards customs and unions. If you and your friend ever founded a startup and your friend cheated you, while you stuck to the contract rules, then you can rest assured that Aryaman will be on your side as he favours honesty. Aryaman will always watch out for you, that is if you

are treading the honest and noble path. Aryaman had a pleasant personality and a fondness for friendships, both promoting and maintaining it.

Aryaman is the son of Aditi and Rishi Kashyapa. He is symbolic of the sun's dharma (his daily rising and setting) and his duty in the universe. Like the sun shines on everything in this cosmos, without partiality, Aryaman blesses everyone equally.

Let me give you a small task. The next time you attend a Hindu marriage ceremony, be present during the *pheras* when the priest is reciting the various mantras. Don't let your thoughts drift to the decorations or the dinner menu, take a pause and pay attention. You will probably hear a hymn with Aryaman's name being chanted to not just invoke him to witness the marriage ceremony but also bless the union of the two people.

There are no hymns solely dedicated or addressed to this solar deity. He is mentioned in the Rig Veda along with Varuna (god of water), Bhaga (god of fortune), and Mitra (god of friendships). Even though Indra was given paramount importance in the Vedic times as he was the most powerful Vedic god, in one of the hymns he seeks gifts and boons from Aryaman. At one time Aryaman was the god of truth, oaths, and contracts, master of knowledge, bestowing wealth and prosperity on people. With the passage of time, all these attributes were absorbed by other gods, so all that was left for Aryaman, the god with the noble looks, known for his chivalry, was to bless the marriage unions.

Did you know that Aryaman was the uncle of Karna, of the Mahabharata fame? As Karna was Surya's spiritual son, it made him Aryaman's nephew. Karna was a big-time worshipper of Surya, his spiritual father, seeking his blessings daily, early in the morning. Like Surya's radiance spreads all over the world, Karna too was known far and wide for his generosity. He had made a pledge that no one would return empty-handed after meeting him. A pledge that cost him his earrings and armour, that were both his shield and strength.

So exalted was Aryaman's status that Lord Krishna in the Bhagavad Gita speaks of himself as being the Bhrigu among the seers, Vyasa among the sages, Vishnu among the children of Aditi, and Aryama (Aryaman) among the departed ancestors. Post the Vedic era, Aryaman was regarded as the divine forefather, the chief of pitrs.

Besides protecting humans, Aryaman is also known to keep the horses safe. He is also symbolic of contracts, agreements, and loyalty. Our galaxy Milky Way is called 'aryamnah panthah,' meaning Aryaman's path.

A mantra to please Aryaman:

Om Aryamayai Namah

Meaning: I bow to Aryaman.

POPULAR BELIEFS

People born under this nakshatra are generous and kind and make good friends, just like Aryaman, the deity of this nakshatra. A friend who is always happy to share their chocolate or brownie is a huge plus. They also have a helpful nature and are reliable, again this is so like Aryaman. So, if you are ever in trouble, it is their number you should dial.

At one time Aryaman had several godly duties, he was given the status of an important deity during the Vedic times. Now Aryaman is just a lovely name, with the deity having long since faded into oblivion.

13

HASTA NAKSHATRA

Deity: Savitr, *The God of Changing Seasons*

According to Vedic astrology, at number thirteen sits the Hasta nakshatra. *Hasta* translates to 'hand.' Sacred hand mudras are often used during meditation to enhance focus and channel energy. Gods held their hands in different mudras conveying blessing, benediction, and protection.

The five stars in the sky that comprise the Hasta nakshatra are Alpha Corvi (Alchiba), Beta Corvi (Kraz), Delta Corvi (Algorab), Gamma Corvi (Gienah), and Epsilon Corvi (Minkar). They are a part of the Corvus constellation. *Corvus* means 'crow' in Latin. When the ancient seers saw this cluster of stars, the pattern they deciphered resembled the five fingertips. Hasta nakshatra also has two other names: Bhanu and Ark (not to be confused with Noah's Ark). If one were to take the literal translation of Bhanu and Ark it would be 'Surya' and 'Surya's rays.'

Let's analyse the three main symbols of this nakshatra. The first is the hand with all the five fingers spread open, like someone is studying the lines on one's palm. The hand is where one's lifelines sit, according to palmistry, the ancient art of reading hands. These lines are believed to be symbolic of our destiny in our current life. Sometimes they are also seen as a sign of hard work. The open hand is symbolic of Surya and the spread fingers represent its rays.

Another symbol of this nakshatra is a clenched fist. A clenched fist cradles in its womb both positive and negative traits. On one side, it is a sign of unity, determination, and fortitude. On the other, it signifies secrecy and a tendency to hide things.

The third symbol is a potter's wheel. A potter, using his hands, shapes the clay on the spinning wheel into beautiful articles. The wheel is also a symbol of passing of time, karma, and transformation.

The ruling planet of this nakshatra is the Moon (Chandra). The luminescent moon plays an important part in Vedic astrology. It shines a light on a person's inner world, influencing the individual's mind, mood, and emotions.

Pulaha is the rishi associated with this nakshatra. His life is symbolic of purity and renunciation. He strictly adhered to religious principles and spiritual practices, becoming a role model for many.

Savitr (or Savitur), the Sun god, is the deity of Hasta nakshatra. The son of Rishi Kashyapa and Aditi, he is one of the Adityas. Savitr is known for his nourishing, inspiring, and life-giving energy. At daybreak, the darkness of the night is lit by a ray of light, like someone has shot a golden arrow, and golden light slowly spreads in all directions soothing and invigorating the world. Savitr's light announces the arrival of a new day full of possibilities.

In the shimmering light appears a golden chariot, drawn by powerful steeds, making its way through the sky. Standing tall in this chariot, which has a golden axle, is the golden-eyed god, his yellow hair flowing, and his golden clothes fluttering in the early morning breeze. Savitr has the ability to assume any form he desires. This god radiates an aura of peace, grace, and an unmatched brilliance that lights up both the heaven and the earth.

Savitr directs the course of the celestial bodies like the sun, moon, and stars. Considered the god of motion, he guides the changing seasons and the passage of days, just like a musician conducts an orchestra, so that there is regularity and rhythm in the cycle of life on earth. No wonder they follow each other seamlessly under his guidance, time after time, for lifetimes.

Savitr has another job, that of bestowing strength and wealth on his devotees and to those who sincerely pray to him. Quite a big responsibility to maintain the Rta, the cosmic order, and sustain life on earth. Savitr also guides the spirits of the departed souls to their correct dwellings in the afterlife. No wonder this deity is always busy.

In spite of all their powers, the gods were many times rendered helpless. Once the Vindhyachal Mountain became jealous of the Sumeru Mountain. It had heard so much about this special mountain, its towering height, its

majestic beauty, its fauna and flora. To compete with the majestic towering peaks of Sumeru and get some praise, Vindhyachal increased its own height, ending up blocking Surya's path in the sky.

As Surya was unable to cross the mountain, Savitr too was stuck and his job couldn't be completed. Half the earth was plunged into day and the other half sunk into night. This continued for days as the mountain refused to budge. Surya's intensity could have burnt the mountain, but out of deference to all the creatures the mountain shielded, Surya refrained from damaging any part of the mountain, preferring to wait for the gods to find another way.

Finally, at Vishnu's behest, the devas appealed to Rishi Agastya. He was a sage known for his wisdom and ingenuity. The sage appeared at the bottom of the Vindhyachal Mountain and started praising it. The mountain felt a sense of pride at the sage's words. Agastya requested the mountain to lower its height as he wanted to travel to the south. His aging body would be unable to cross the mountain's enormous height. He further appealed to the mountain that it should not raise itself until the sage returned from his journey of the southern regions.

Vindhyachal was more than eager to oblige the learned sage. It immediately lowered its height, allowing both the sage and the Sun god to move. Daylight pierced the earth and the sage made his way to the south, easily traversing the lowered peaks of the mountain. At the god's behest, the sage had hoodwinked the mountain. Rishi Agastya settled down in the south and Vindhyachal is still awaiting the sage's return.

Most people are unaware that the sun before sunrise is called Savitr and the daylight sun, Surya. This makes Savitr an aspect of the sun that removes the darkness of the night. Eleven hymns of the Rig Veda pay obeisance to Savitr with a total of one hundred and seventy mentions.

Savitr was revered during the Vedic period as a powerful deity. But after the Vedic period, the Trinity – Shiva, Brahma, and Vishnu – who were less popular during early times when people worshipped the sakshat gods (the visible gods) like the sun, moon, rain, fire, wind became central. These sakshat gods had more power as they were responsible for feeding the people by influencing crops and affecting the outcome of the harvest.

Though less popular now, with people puzzling over his identity, Savitr is invoked in the Gayatri mantra. His divine energy flows into those who chant the mantra with devotion, guiding them in all spheres of life, especially when they want to go beyond the material world, into the blissful spiritual realm.

Want to learn the Gayatri mantra?

Om bhur bhuvah svah
Tat savitur varenyam
Bhargo devasya Dhimahi
Dhiyo yo nah prachodayat
Rig Veda 3.62.10

Meaning: O thou existence absolute (O Divine creator), creator of the three dimensions (physical, mental, and spiritual), we meditate upon thy divine light. May the darkness from our intellect be removed and true knowledge bestowed upon us.

POPULAR BELIEFS

People born under this nakshatra love to laugh and joke and also make others laugh. Humour is their strong point and they are light-hearted in nature. But they also have a practical approach to life. It is believed that Savitr had a jovial and light-hearted nature, and enjoyed playing games. This personality trait of the deity could seep down to the people born under this nakshatra.

Just like Savitr has accepted his job of announcing the sun's arrival and creating the path for the Sun god's chariot in the sky, we should all accept the challenges and obstacles life throws our way and go about our work with sincerity and dedication.

14

CHITRA NAKSHATRA

Deity: Vishwakarma, *The Divine Architect*

Chitra is a beautiful name that we all have heard many times. Perhaps some of us may even have friends with this name. The word *chitra*, the name of the fourteenth nakshatra, means 'bright,' 'art,' 'glittering,' 'brilliant,' 'beautiful,' 'visual,' and even 'magic.' Those born under this nakshatra imbibe many of these qualities.

This nakshatra is associated with a single star: Spica. Also known as Alpha Virginis, it is one of the brightest stars in the star-studded night sky, visible even in the lightly polluted skies. It lies in the Virgo constellation.

With a single bright star representing this nakshatra, it is only befitting that its main symbol is a shining jewel or a pearl.

Planet Mars (Mangal) rules over this nakshatra. Mars has two small, potato-shaped moons called Phobos and

Deimos. They always show the same face to the planet, just like Earth's Moon.

Rishi Kratu is associated with this nakshatra. One of the mind-born sons of Brahma, Rishi Kratu was invited for the birth celebrations of Kartikeya (Shiva and Parvati's son).

Vishwakarma (also known as Tvasta or Tvastar, the divine architect) is the deity of this nakshatra. Born from Brahma's mind, Vishwakarma, like his father, was also engaged in creation. He built things inside the universe created by Brahma – celestial palaces, divine chariots, and weapons. His designs were a marvel of architecture and the wonders of the cosmic world. This architect of the devas was a much sought-after craftsman. Vishwakarma finds his name mentioned five times in the tenth book of the Rig Veda. That shows his power and prestige.

Beauty was the hallmark of his designs. It is believed that Vishwakarma was responsible for the final look of Surya. At Surya's urging, this divine architect doubled as his makeover artist, helping dim Surya's glow.

This talented god is a beautiful sight to behold. He is depicted having four hands, a crown adorns his head and he wears loads of gold jewellery (he must have designed the jewellery himself). In his hands he holds a book, a waterpot, a noose, and craftsman's tools. This deity seems to have been working tirelessly through the yugas. In the Satya Yuga, he built the Swarga loka – the heavenly realm where gods and demigods lived. In the Treta Yuga, he made the golden city of Lanka, aka Sone ki Lanka, which was coveted by many. In the Dwapara Yuga, he created the city of Dwarka for Lord Krishna, and Hastinapur, the capital of the Kuru dynasty.

There is a story in the Ramayana about Vishwakarma that few will know. After Shiva married Parvati, he requested Vishwakarma to build a beautiful city and palace for them to live in. Vishwakarma was delighted. Building something for Mahadeva was a dream come true. As it was a residence for Shiva, Vishwakarma put his heart and soul into the construction and built a palace and city made of gold. This palace glowed like thousand suns. The entire city looked splendid. The roads glittered and the buildings gleamed. In time the city and the palace were ready for Shiva and Parvati to settle in.

Before moving in, Shiva wanted to do a *grihapravesham*, the housewarming ceremony. He invited Ravana, who was renowned for his wisdom, to perform the ceremony. Ravana was more than happy to do the ceremony as it was a matter of prestige for him. Ravana performed the rituals sincerely. After they were over, as per the custom, Shiva offered Ravana a *dakshina* (gift or fee). He could ask for anything he wanted. Thoroughly enchanted with the beauty and grandeur of the palace, he asked for the golden palace itself as dakshina. Shiva granted it to him without hesitation. Ravana lived in the golden palace that became Lanka, ruling over the city. After being killed by Rama, Ravana's brother Vibhishana was entrusted with its care.

Another story attributes Lanka to have been made by Vishwakarma for the demons Mali and Sumali. After Vishnu slayed Mali and overthrew Sumali, Brahma made Kubera the ruler of Lanka as Kubera had prayed fervently to Brahma for gold. Kubera's half-brothers, Ravana and Kumbhakarna, wrested Lanka from Kubera.

One might assume that the divine architect would restrict his masterpieces to heaven. But this clever and talented architect decided to spread his wings far and wide, to all the lokas – Prithvi, Patala, and Swarga.

When Indra rose to power as king of the devas, the god turned to Vishwakarma for something befitting a ruler of the skies. Vishwakarma delivered. Not only did he craft Indra's magnificent palace, but he also forged the mighty thunderbolt, Indra's signature weapon, powerful enough to shatter mountains.

And where Indra is mentioned, can Kubera be far behind? The god of wealth needed a residence as lavish as his treasures. Vishwakarma answered with a masterpiece – Kubera's palace near Alakapuri, surrounded by gardens so enchanting they'd make any earthly paradise look ordinary.

Varuna, the water god, didn't want to be left out where the race for beautiful palaces was concerned. The water god's request resulted in Vishwakarma building a gorgeous underwater palace called Shraddhavati, with its stunning all-round views.

Seeing all the beautiful abodes, Yama decided his city of Yamapuri in Patala loka, the netherworld, too needed a palace that would make people stop and admire. People in their afterlife could do with some good visuals. Who other than Vishwakarma could do that? So, he approached Vishwakarma to construct his official palace.

When the Pandavas wanted to build their city of Indraprastha, Lord Krishna approached Vishwakarma to lend his skills into constructing the beautiful city that would be the stuff of peoples' dreams.

POPULAR BELIEFS

People born under this nakshatra have a strong sense of aesthetics. They also love to find out how things work. They are balls of energy and can never stay still, they need to be constantly on the move, always doing something or the other. These traits are so reminiscent of Vishwakarma, his eye for beautiful designs was legendary, and he was constantly building new things.

Vishwakarma's life shows us that dedication and hard work are necessary at every stage. One can't rest on past glories as each new work is a fresh opportunity to prove one's worth, and each new task is a fresh challenge that must be overcome. That constant endeavour for excellence is the only way of life.

15

SWATI NAKSHATRA

Deity: Vayu, *The Multifaceted God*

Swati in Sanskrit translates to 'delicate,' 'tender,' 'independent,' and 'sword.' The last meaning is completely opposite of the first two and so different from the third. Perhaps pointing to the multi-faceted aspect of this star and its characteristics.

Arcturus, or Alpha Boötis, is the star representing this nakshatra. It is the fourth-brightest star in the night sky, visible even through a layer of smog and dust, and is part of the Boötes constellation. This single star impressed the ancient Vedic sages to such an extent that they attributed to it the status of Saraswati's abode, the reclusive goddess of learning, music, and knowledge.

A tender young shoot blown by the wind is one of the symbols of this nakshatra. Young plants carry with them a sense of delicateness and fragility. Now you get the connotation with the words tender and delicate? Another symbol of this nakshatra is the beautiful coral. The third symbol is a sword. A sword has a sharp and a fierce quality to it. It can cut, and is used for protection.

Rahu (North Lunar Node) is the ruling planet of this nakshatra. In Sanskrit, *Raa* or *Rah* means to hide or something that is hidden. Bhayanka is the other name of Rahu. Sounds scary, doesn't it? The time of the day that comes under the influence of Rahu is known as Rahu Kala or Rahu Kalam, and it is not considered a good time to start auspicious events.

Marichi is the rishi associated with this nakshatra. One of the seven great sages, Marichi has been credited with guiding Dhruva, the young boy, when he wanted to perform penance to please Vishnu.

Vayu, the god of wind, is the deity of this nakshatra. His arrival is felt before it is seen: Leaves rustle, dust swirls, clothes flutter, as Vayu, sitting in his beautiful, shiny chariot drawn by white and purple horses, races across the skies beneath a rippling white banner.

He is a multi-faceted god. He can be the warm gentle breeze caressing one's skin, or a gust of cold mountain air. He can be the quiet air you breathe or a howling typhoon trying to wreak havoc. He is seldom portrayed as a quiet deity and is mostly attributed to destructive forces. He is considered both powerful and a fighter.

Vayu was born from the breath of Vishvapurusha, the Supreme Being. The word *vayu* means 'air' or 'wind,' the vital life force. When he isn't travelling in his chariot, he

rides his gazelle to move from one place to another. In his omnipresent form as the wind, he roams all over the world, freely. Your eyes can't see him, but his soft whispers against your skin point to his presence.

During the Vedic times, Vayu had the honour of having the first sip of Soma along with Indra. While they enjoyed the first drink like good friends, the other deities watched them enviously.

With power comes confidence, and Vayu possessed loads of it. A tale narrates Vayu's competition with Vasuki, the king of snakes, to decide who was more powerful. Vasuki coiled himself around a mountain. Vayu could not budge Vasuki. The snake could not escape Vayu's hold on him. It was a stalemate with two powerful opponents not conceding an inch. Only the poor mountain bore the brunt of this competition, suffering an onslaught from both the snake and the god of wind. Ultimately, Lord Vishnu had to intervene and end the contest. Not wanting to antagonize Vishnu, Vasuki uncoiled from the mountain. The moment he did that; the smart god of wind blew with such a force that the mountain's peak ripped off and its base shook. Vayu threw this mountain to the far south, where it landed in the vast ocean. Can you guess which place is this? A clue. It features in the Ramayana. Yes, you are right, it is the beautiful island of Sri Lanka, the land of Ravana.

Vayu had two spiritual sons: Hanuman and Bhima. They have kept him alive in the hearts and minds of the people down the ages. The powerful Hanuman, unmatched in strength and in his devotion to Lord Rama, is also known as Pawanaputra (Pawan is another name of Vayu) and Vayuputra.

There is a beautiful story about Vayu and his son Hanuman. One day, young Hanuman mistook the sun for a fruit. So, typical of a young child, Hanuman attempted to eat the sun. This innocent act made the other gods fearful and they all thought that he was a demon. Indra, armed with his powerful weapon, the famous Vajra, attacked the child. The Vajra not just injured Hanuman but also rendered him unconscious, making him fall down to earth.

Vayu caught Hanuman, preventing his fall. Furious with the other gods for attacking his child and injuring him, Vayu did the unthinkable. He withdrew the air in the universe. It was nothing short of a catastrophe. Everyone (humans, animals, birds, plants, and other creatures) started suffocating and collapsing due to lack of air. The gods watched helplessly, unable to do anything to save anyone. They did what they always did when faced with a problem – rushed to one of the trinities for a solution.

Brahma realized the impact this would have on the universe. He requested Vayu to resume the air so people and animals could breathe again. But Vayu was adamant. Brahma then healed Hanuman of his injuries, bringing him back to consciousness. As Vayu restored the air, things returned to normal. The gods accompanying Brahma bestowed many boons and blessings on Hanuman.

Hanuman, though powerful, was not even aware of his strength, so absorbed was he in his devotion to Lord Rama. He played several important roles in Rama's search for Sita and his subsequent battle with Ravana.

Vayu was Bhima's (one of the Pandavas) spiritual father, too. Bhima's mother, Kunti, had prayed to Vayu to bless her with a powerful and strong son. Bhima's strength and prowess with the mace was legendary and his skill exemplary. Like Hanuman, Bhima too was known for his strength and power. But unlike Hanuman, Bhima wasn't humble and was well aware of his might and strength. The Kurukshetra War fought between the Pandavas and the Kauravas owes a lot to Bhima's skill with the mace.

Vayu's exalted status diminished post the Vedic period and he was relegated to the status of a dikpala, a guardian of the north-west direction.

POPULAR BELIEFS

People born under this nakshatra seldom take sides, preferring a neutral route just like Vayu. They are hard-working, goal-oriented, and are always eager to learn something new, be it an art or a new way of thinking. They can also be good procrastinators, like the classmate who has been postponing their homework till the last minute, when the teacher asks for it.

Vayu is crucial to all forms of life. No creature can survive without it, even for a few minutes. It is said that whenever Vishnu and Lakshmi travelled, Vayu travelled along with them.

16

VISHAKHA NAKSHATRA

Deity: Indra and Agni, *The Gods Who Liked to Test Their Devotees*

At the sixteenth position is Vishakha nakshatra. The Sanskrit word *vishakha* means 'forked' or 'two-branched.' But the third meaning, 'poison vessel,' makes one frown. Perhaps in that poison vessel meaning, it is the *vish* part of the word *vishakha* that's in focus. The nakshatra has another name: Radha. Though *radha* means delightful, success, or prosperity, this name is more famous for its association with Lord Krishna's ardent and supreme devotee Radha.

This nakshatra is represented by four stars in the Libra constellation: Alpha Librae, Beta Librae, Gamma Librae and Iota Librae. Alpha Librae, also known as Zubenelgenubi (it means southern claw in Arabic), and Beta Librae, also called Zubeneschamali (northern claw), are the brightest of the lot. The ancient seers saw the four stars of this nakshatra forming a forked branch. They immediately jotted it down as being connected to Indra, considering it an abode of the gods, under Indra's rule.

The main symbol of this nakshatra is a decorated or triumphant arch, or a gateway. But as this arch or gateway is decorated with leaves, it symbolizes a ceremony or a celebration. Another symbol of Vishakha is two branches, which ties back to its name.

Jupiter (Brihaspati) is the ruling planet of this nakshatra. It spins really fast, making it look oblate. The planet takes just about nine hours and fifty minutes to turn on its axis, resulting in it having the shortest day among the planets. That's shorter than a full night's beauty sleep for many people!

Vashishta is the rishi associated with this nakshatra. Considered by many as the first sage of the Vedanta School of Hindu philosophy, Vashishta is believed to have written Mandala 7 of the Rig Veda. It has 104 hymns.

This nakshatra has not one but two main deities: Indra and Agni. Indragni. Indra is associated with thunder and storm, and Agni with heat and fire. Both these gods enjoyed testing their devotees. The devotees always had to be on alert mode; ever ready to undergo a harsh test at the drop of a hat.

One day, Indra and Agni decided to test a king named Shibi. The king, a devotee of Vishnu, was the son of the

Chandravanshi (lunar dynasty) king Ushinara. Wise and benevolent, always treading the right path, he was known for his kindness and generosity. His fame spread far and wide, reaching the gods of heaven. Indra, the lord of heaven, wanted to check if what he had heard about Shibi was true or just rumours. Taking Agni into confidence, he made a plan and decided to test the king.

Both the gods transformed themselves: Agni into a pigeon and Indra into a hawk. In this new guise, the hawk began to chase the pigeon. The pigeon approached Shibi standing in the garden of his palace. The pigeon appealed to the king to protect him from the hawk chasing him. The kind king promised the pigeon protection. Once Shibi's promise was made, the hawk approached the king and demanded that the pigeon be given to him as it would feed his famished family. The king, adamant about protecting the pigeon, refused. The hawk insisted saying that he had been pursuing it for some time. Once again, the king refused. The insistent hawk now demanded from the king a part of his thigh equivalent to the pigeon's body, so that his starving family could have their meal. The king agreed.

Most people wouldn't have parted with even a strand of their hair, but Shibi was different. He asked his men to bring a scale. Once the scale was set, the king placed the pigeon on one side, and cutting a piece of his thigh for the hawk, placed it on the other. Much to his surprise, the large chunk of his flesh weighed less than the pigeon. So Shibi carved out some more flesh from his legs. But no matter how much flesh the king added, the pigeon was always heavier.

Finally, the wounded king decided that he would sit on the scale himself. The moment he did, the birds transformed into Agni and Indra. They were stunned by the king's kindness and sacrifice. Indra and Agni showered several blessings on Shibi and brought him to heaven as a reward for his generosity.

We often hear about Indra – his character traits, his personality. But his wife, Indrani, the Queen of the Gods, was no less powerful. She matched her husband in smartness. They were a perfect couple, made for each other. Indrani, a goddess with 'endless beauty' and radiant skin according to the Rig Veda, had one thousand eyes; each eye was captivating. The number of her arms vary, from two to four to even six. Like her husband, she too is associated with an elephant, but keeping her Devi- or Shakti-like persona, it is not a sedentary white elephant but a charging one. Sometimes she rides a lion. She carries a thunderbolt or a vajra, and because she is attributed as having more arms, she carries several other objects: a noose (doesn't it remind you of Yama?), a lotus stalk (a Saraswati connection), and a goad. Like the other goddesses, she is adorned with many ornaments keeping her celestial status in mind and the pride of place in her jewellery is her Kirita Mukuta (the highest of crowns).

Daughter of an asura named Puloman whom Indra killed, Indrani is associated with a whole lot of intense traits and is considered the goddess of jealousy, anger, and wrath. But this doesn't imply that she gives people jealousy. In fact, it is the opposite – she destroys the enviousness people experience. She has a hymn dedicated to her in the Rig Veda, and also has several names: Sachi (sometimes spelt as Shachi), Aindri, Poulomi (a derivative of her father's name Puloman), Vajri, Mahendri, and Pulomaja (also derived from Puloman).

POPULAR BELIEFS

People born under this nakshatra are highly focused and determined in pursuing their goals. Their dedication and single-mindedness help them achieve great things, reflecting the traits of Indra, who was known for his strong commitment to his power, position, and responsibilities, and his unwavering resolve to protect them. This resolve is further amplified by the willpower and courage of Agni, granting them strength to overpower any obstacles in their way.

Indra and Agni weren't just content with seeing their devotees' faith, devotion, and prayers, they also liked to test their faith and devotion and see how much goodness they had imbibed and how much goodness they were spreading in the world. They did this by assuming many disguises and putting their devotees to different tests.

17

ANURADHA NAKSHATRA

Deity: Mitra, *The BFF Everyone Wants*

At the seventeenth place is Anuradha nakshatra. Anuradha means 'another Radha' or even 'after Radha.' In English it takes on the meaning of 'subsequent success.' Jog your memory a wee bit and go back to the previous nakshatra, Vishakha, and remember its association with Radha, the great devotee of Krishna. Perhaps Radha's devotion finds its culmination in this nakshatra. Some scholars and sages considered Vishakha and Anuradha a pair, maybe it was due to this connection with Radha.

This nakshatra is represented in the sky by three stars: Beta Scorpii (Acrab), Delta Scorpii (Dschubba), and Pi Scorpii (Fang). Beta Scorpii is the brightest of the three, just like a class topper. This trio of stars can be found at the beginning of the Scorpius constellation. When the ancient sages saw the three stars of this nakshatra, making a slight curve, they immediately decoded it to be the shape of a staff. Hence a staff is the main symbol of this nakshatra. Staffs can be quite powerful. In the Puranas, the sages are always depicted as carrying a staff. This staff is not just a simple wooden stick but a receptacle of their power, as all the penances they have done has made the staff a force to reckon with. The staff was a sage's ultimate protection, used only in emergencies and for self-defence.

The other symbol of this nakshatra is a lotus. Considered pure and auspicious, it is associated with knowledge and enlightenment. It is not just the seat of Saraswati, the goddess of learning, and Lakshmi, the goddess of wealth, many gods are depicted as holding a lotus flower in one of their hands. A lotus is used as an example for how it grows in muddy waters yet retains its purity and remains untouched by its surroundings. There is a third symbol which is a victory arch or a triumphal archway.

Saturn (Shani) is the ruling planet of this nakshatra. It travels around the Sun once in every 29.4 Earth years. The ancient Assyrians gave it the nickname 'Lubadsagush' (meaning oldest of the old) because of its slow movement.

Angiras is the rishi associated with this nakshatra. He had exceptional singing talent, constantly singing hymns in praise of the Trinity, and mesmerizing the gods as well as the humans with his voice.

With such lovely symbols attached to it, the deity of this nakshatra, too, has to be sweet and benevolent. It is Mitra, the Vedic god who rules over friendships, cordiality, warmth, and good faith. Everyone knows the meaning of *mitra* – a friend. If one doesn't have this deity's blessings, one can never make friends, forget best friends. Mitra is one of the twelve Adityas (solar deities), son of Rishi Kashyapa and Aditi.

Riding on his chariot pulled by horses, this endearing god, with a gentle look on his face, spread his magic, fusing friends together. Mitra himself loves friendships. Whenever one invokes him for blessings or mentions his name, there is always an invocation that involves his two friends – the water god, Varuna, and his sibling, Aryaman. Having a sibling who doubles as a friend is the best thing that can happen to anyone, as then there would be no one sneaking to the parents about the cookies you secretly gobbled before dinner or the tub of chocolate ice cream you devoured at midnight, as you would have a partner in crime to do all this.

Coming back to Mitra, his BFF is Varuna. Mitra's name is almost always taken along with Varuna, they are usually addressed as Mitra-Varuna, often invoked together as a pair. One would have seen them roaming heaven together, sharing secrets and confiding in each other. Mitra is youthful-looking, stylishly dressed in regal and elegant clothes, lives in a golden palace that is said to have a thousand pillars and a thousand doors. (The palace must be super huge and may need a vehicle, a kind of a buggy, to move around from one room to another!) His godly duties make him the guardian of the entire world as friendship is the key to survival.

Mitra and Varuna are believed to be incharge of Rta, the moral and cosmic order. You could think of them as cosmic police officers. In the Atharvaveda, Mitra has been linked to sunrise. Hindus invoke him during their morning upasana or upasthana prayers. Mitra bestows knowledge, awareness, and harmony. Varuna, on the other hand, relates to the evening and night.

But sometimes even enemies act as friends, if they can achieve a common goal by coming together for a certain time or some purpose. Remember the Samudra Manthan or the churning of the ocean where the devas and asuras, arch enemies, constantly at war, came together to churn the ocean for the nectar of immortality? We can safely assume that this was all done under the blessings of the deity Mitra, who for the duration of that task, made the devas and asuras drop their animosity and accept a truce. Because only by coming together the devas and asuras could achieve what they wouldn't have been able to do alone. Churn the ocean. So, if you had a tiff with your best friend and want to patch up, Mitra is just a sincere prayer away.

For any friendship to flourish, Mitra's blessings are needed. It was Mitra's blessings showered upon Sudama that made him forge a friendship with Krishna. Krishna and Sudama's story continues to be narrated down the ages as a mark of true friendship. The two *sakha*s (friends) studied together at Rishi Sandipani's hermitage, and despite the difference in their status formed an enduring bond. Sudama was seeped in poverty while Krishna was living in the lap of luxury in the beautiful city of Dwarka. One day, at his wife's insistence, Sudama arrived in Krishna's palace, carrying with him a handful of puffed rice as a gift, to ask for his friend's help to get him out of poverty.

Krishna was delighted to see his childhood friend. While Sudama ate the delicious spread Krishna's staff laid out for him, Krishna was content to eat the puffed rice his friend had brought for him. The puffed rice transported him to childhood, making him relive his gurukul days. A few days later, Sudama left his friend's palace, unable to ask him for help.

He walked home, his eyes filled with tears, saddened that he hadn't done what his wife had asked him. As he approached his house, his mouth went dry and his heart beat wildly. His humble hut had disappeared, and in its place he saw a palace. From inside this glorious palace, his wife and son emerged. Instead of their usually dull rags, they were dressed in finery. In the blink of an eye, Krishna had changed Sudama's family's fortunes. He had fulfilled the hidden desire of his childhood friend and repaid the handful of puffed rice he had eaten from his friend.

Along with his friendship duties, Mitra was the god of oaths, sacred promises, contracts, and meetings. Mitra is said to have a thousand eyes and with these he can single out people who will break their oaths and promises. Next time you and your friend make a promise, invoke Mitra, beseeching him to help you. These thousand eyes are supposed to be the thousand stars in the sky that have fabulous scanning ability, like an X-ray, which can easily identify the promise breakers and liars. So, if your friend is lying to you, Mitra will help you out.

POPULAR BELIEFS

People born under this nakshatra are logical, loyal, disciplined, and think deeply. They also possess a good intuition, just like Mitra does when he forges friendships and bonds by bringing together people who will help each other in the longer run. That's really a huge blessing as a sharp intuition can make you aware of trouble and troublemakers. People born under this star can be both friendly and aloof, as and when the situation demands it.

Mitra's blessings are important as life without friends is like living in a vacuum. And if this deity is being extra generous, one gets a special BFF and many lovely friends who are more like soulmates than friends.

18

JYESHTA NAKSHATRA

Deity: Indra, *The God with a Temper*

The meaning of the eighteenth nakshatra, Jyeshta, is 'eldest' and 'senior most.' It is believed that initially there were just eighteen nakshatras, and Jyeshta was the senior most or the eldest one. But once more nakshatras were added, Jyeshta lost that position, but the name remained the same.

This nakshatra consists of a trio of stars in the Scorpius constellation: Alpha Scorpii, Sigma Scorpii, and Tau Scorpii. Alpha Scorpii is commonly known as Antares, Sigma Scorpii as Alniyat, and Tau Scorpii as Paikauhale. According to the ancient seers, these stars seem to form the pattern of an earring or the top portion of an umbrella. The brightest star in the constellation, the reddish-hued Antares, is nicknamed the 'Scorpion's Heart.' It can be spotted easily in the night sky, and was revered by people of the ancient times.

Jyeshta nakshatra is also symbolized by a round talisman or amulet. Talismans signify divine protection. They also enjoy a status of authority and power. In olden times, kings wore round talismans resembling medallions, and large round earrings. A circle represents an endless cycle, like every part of nature. Day merges into night, which again merges into day and so on, endlessly. Seasons repeat. The cycle of life and death is ongoing.

The ruling planet of this nakshatra is Mercury (Budha). It is the smallest planet in our solar system, and has a rocky surface and a thin exosphere (this is the outermost layer of a planet's atmosphere), which was formed when atoms blasted off its surface due to strong solar winds and meteoroids striking it.

The rishi associated with this nakshatra is Atri. Atri and his wife, Anasuya, were known for their piousness, tapasya, and hospitality. They made an ideal couple and were high on the list of the most-respected rishi-couple.

With all these prestigious symbols attached to it, it doesn't surprise one that Indra is the deity associated with this nakshatra. Mention Indra, and the first thing that comes to mind is his obsession with his throne. The eldest son of Mother Goddess Aditi and Rishi Kashyapa, he was the ruler of heaven and the king of gods. More powerful than all the prime ministers and presidents of the world. If anyone engaged in intense tapasya or austerities, Indra immediately became insecure and started worrying that his throne was in jeopardy. He would assume different forms and do his best to break their meditation so they couldn't achieve their goals or aims.

Indra was a proud deity, but for all his power and pride, he always needed help of one of the gods whenever trouble approached him. In the Srimad Bhagavatam, there is a story about Indra. Once a powerful demon named Narakasura attacked heaven. He took Indra's royal umbrella and his mother, Aditi's, earrings. Indra, like always, approached Lord Krishna for help. The generous god, along with his

wife Satyabhama, sitting astride Garuda – the powerful eagle – arrived at Indra's palace and waged a battle with Narakasura. After defeating the demon, Krishna retrieved the stolen umbrella and earrings from him, and promptly returned them to Indra and his mother.

A grateful Indra requested Krishna and his wife to enjoy his hospitality and the beauty of his palace as a token of his gratitude. Aditi – not to be left behind in the gratitude department – taught many art forms to Satyabhama.

The Puranas refer to Indra as an angry god, intoxicated with his power and prestige, sending heavy rains on earth whenever he was in a grumpy mood. Indra tried the same trick with a young Krishna, forgetting that he was dealing with a powerful god who could make things happen in the blink of an eye.

The Srimad Bhagavatam recounts another such story about Indra. One day, the six-year-old Krishna saw his father and the people of Vrindavan preparing for a yagna to appease Indra. Krishna questioned the ritual, arguing that it was nature, the forests of the Govardhana Hill, which were responsible for giving them food and providing nourishment to their cows. He convinced the elders that instead of performing the sacrifice in Indra's honour, they should use all the resources they had saved for the yagna for the welfare of the animals and nature.

Indra was furious that the yagna in his honour wasn't being done. Summoning his most powerful storms, he directed them at Vrindavan. There was a torrential downpour that threatened to flood the village. The villagers, fearing Indra's wrath, beseeched Krishna for protection. Krishna prayed to the Govardhana Hill and lifted it on the little finger of his left hand, like an umbrella, and all the villagers rushed to take shelter under it. Indra's rage lasted for seven days.

This feat of the young boy made Indra realize that he was none other than Vishnu. Indra stopped the storms and rushed to the village to seek forgiveness from Krishna, taking with him the gift of the cows of heaven. Cows were Krishna's favourite animals. Accepting the gift, the soft-hearted boy immediately forgave Indra. A relieved Indra went back to heaven.

For all his weaknesses, Indra makes for an awe-inspiring visual. Carrying a thunderbolt in his hands, he rides his majestic white elephant, Airavata. Eons back, Indra commanded lot of respect and was highly revered and worshipped. Around 250 hymns in the Rig Veda are dedicated to Indra, a testimony to the powerful status he enjoyed in the pantheon of gods. But in later texts, the focus shifted to the Trinity (Brahma, Vishnu, Shiva) and Indra was seen more as a symbol of power and his influence over the weather. He was considered as king of heaven and leader of the devas.

POPULAR BELIEFS

People born under Jyeshta nakshatra are very aware of how others perceive them and are keenly attuned to their surroundings. They have a flair for the dramatic and enjoy expressing themselves, and they are also highly competitive. This competitive spirit is reflected in Indra, who was always alert to strong rivals and used his cleverness to stay ahead.

Indra's life is a testimony to the fact that with great power also comes great insecurity. A case of uneasy lies the head that wears the crown. While the other gods relaxed in their heavenly abodes, Indra was a bundle of nerves, always worried that someone would steal his kingdom and stake a claim over his palace and position.

19

MULA NAKSHATRA

Deity: Nirriti, *The Goddess of Disorder and Chaos*

Mula means 'root,' 'innermost core,' or even 'centre.' Number nineteen in the list of nakshatras, Mula nakshatra carries a lot of weight in its essence.

Nine stars represent this nakshatra in the sky: Lambda Scorpii, Epsilon Scorpii, Mu[1] Scorpii, Iota[1] Scorpii, Theta Scorpii, Eta Scorpii, Zeta Scorpii, Kappa Scorpii, and Upsilon Scorpii. The formal name of Lambda Scorpii is Shaula, Epsilon Scorpii is Larawag, Mu[1] Scorpii is Xamidimura, Iota[1] Scorpii is Apollyon, Theta Scorpii is Sargas, Kappa Scorpii is Girtab, and Upsilon Scorpii is Lesath. Eta and Zeta Scorpii do not have any proper names. According to the ancient sages, these stars resemble the shape of a lion's tail. While many believe it resembles the tail of a scorpion. This description fits more than the lion's tail one.

Shaula and Lesath are known as the 'stinger stars' because these stars can be found in the tail of Scorpius constellation. While Shaula takes pride in being the second-brightest star of the Scorpius constellation, Lesath is the fainter star and these two stinger stars are separated by nearly five light years.

The main symbol of this nakshatra is a tied bunch of roots, which aligns with the name Mula. Though the roots of trees aren't visible, they go deep underground and provide the tree with the required nourishment. They also grow and spread far and wide, just likes the tree's branches visible above the soil.

The ruling planet of this nakshatra is Ketu (South Lunar Node). Ketu is considered the ninth navagraha – the nine planets in Hindu astrology. A shadow planet, it has no physical existence or presence.

Pulastya is the rishi associated with this nakshatra. A rishi wielding considerable clout, he performed austerities and penance on the slopes of Mount Meru.

A small shiver of apprehension might ripple through the readers when they learn about the deity of Mula nakshatra: Nirriti, whose name means 'calamity.' Nirriti's arrival is the stuff of a dystopian fantasy.

An eerie atmosphere prevails in the kingdom of darkness and the dead. There is a chill in the air that freezes one's blood and paralyses one's limbs. Eerie whispers fill the air. There is chaos and disorder. Rakshasas and rakshasis swarm the place. Dark clouds thicken the gloom, and in the darkness, shapes shift restlessly, as though awaiting some kind of instruction.

In the shadowy darkness, a silhouette emerges. Silence falls as she moves. The dark clouds part, and light casts its illuminating glow on the figure making its way out of the kingdom of the dead.

A deity wearing black clothes becomes visible. Her gold ornaments shine, drawing attention to her presence. Sitting astride her vahana, the donkey, though some say it is a lion and others say it is a man, she surveys her surroundings. Owls and pigeons fly all around her. The pigeons are her messengers and await her instructions. Nirriti, the Vedic goddess of chaos, has started her journey. With a name that translates to 'absence of Rta (divine order),' this goddess of darkness, destruction, misery, old age, fear, decay, and calamity, brings with her pain, misfortune, and death wherever she goes.

In the distance, she can hear the chanting of the mantras. The air echoes with hundreds of voices reciting after the priests. Smoke from the sacrificial fire, the yagna kund, weaves its way upwards making strange patterns.

Nirriti moves soundlessly towards the place of the sacrificial yagna. As the chants and Vedic rituals beseeching her to keep away fill the air, she respectfully stops. So do the pigeons and the owls. She always responds to sincere prayers requesting her to stay away from yagnas and sacrifices and not taint them with her presence, which is considered inauspicious. She knows that there will be an offering left for her after the yagna.

She waits at the periphery of the holy ritual, bidding her time until she can partake the yagna offerings. Her vahana surveys the site, its eyes gleaming at the pile of offerings. The deity's eyes move over the yagna site where Rta spreads its disciplined presence, not allowing disorder and chaos to put a toe in the wrong place.

After the yagna is over and the gods appeased, people start leaving. Soon the yagna site looks deserted. Wisps of lazy smoke curl up from the dying embers.

Nirriti now pats her donkey. It moves forward. Nirriti's eyes shine as she spies the offering left for her. True to her nature, dark husks are what she will take. After she has partaken the offering, her vahana turns around under her telepathic instructions. The owls and pigeons follow, and the group makes its way back to the kingdom of the dead.

This Vedic deity's parents, Adharma (unrighteousness) and Himsa (violence), and her children Bhaya (fear), Mahabhaya (terror), and Mrityu (death) will make you fearful.

Nirriti is mentioned a few times in the Rig Veda and other sacred texts. These Rig Vedic hymns describing her nature actually beg her to depart from a place, especially a sacrificial site, so that goodness and prosperity can prevail. Else with her presence, the auspicious will keep away.

A story in the Puranas gives Nirriti the title of Alakshmi (misfortune) requesting her in the Sri Sukta mantra:

Kshut-pipasa-malam jyestham alaksmim nasayamyaham,
abhutim asamrddhim ca sarvam nirnuda me grihat.

Meaning:

O Jatavedo, I invoke the Lakshmi whose presence destroys hunger, thirst, illness, misfortune, and impurity associated with her elder sister Alakshmi. I beseech her to remove ill-fortune and misery from my house.

According to some Vedic texts, she is depicted as a demoness, while others present her as Alakshmi, the goddess of poverty, misfortune, and calamity. This sister of Lakshmi dislikes prosperity and abundance and presides over sorrows, miseries, decay, destruction, and ruin. But before fear sets in at the mention of Nirriti, it is important to remember that not just Nirriti, but none of the gods – whether associated with fortune or misfortune – punish randomly. Nirriti watches over our karma. She keeps a sharp eye out for sinners. Bad karmic deeds equal sorrows and miseries. So, if you have been good, there is nothing to fear.

A mantra to appease this deity:

Om Shree Mata Nirriti Deviye Namah

There is a general belief that while worshipping Nirriti, all the offerings made to her should only be taken by the priests performing the ceremony. The people are allowed only to smell these offerings as eating them will be inauspicious. It is also said that after funeral ceremonies, where Nirriti and Rudra are present, people should just walk away, without looking back or around, as that may be considered an invitation for Nirriti to follow them.

If you pray to her with faith and devotion, she relieves one of sorrows and miseries and unnatural death. As a bonus, she removes the fear of death and bad thoughts, and transforms enemies into friends.

If you want to see a statue of this deity, the famous Rajarani temple in Bhubaneswar holds a statue of Nirriti guarding the south-west direction. She stands over a prostrate body, holding a sword and a severed head in her hands.

Nirriti's birth is mentioned in the Mahabharata.

Brahma sat down in the lotus posture and meditated. His creation was at its peak – his creative energy overflowing from both his mind and body. As he entered deeper and deeper into meditation, the air itself throbbed with anticipation of what would come next. From his lap emerged Narada. Prajapati Daksha came out from his right thumb. As Brahma breathed, Vashishta appeared from the creator's breath. From the creator's skin came out Bhrigu. Kratu crawled out from his hand. From the navel Pulaha slipped out. From his ear, Pulastya made an appearance. From the mouth dropped Angiras. From the eye slid Atri. From the mind came Marichi. Dharma emerged from his right breast. Adharma rippled out from his back. From the creator's heart, Kama appeared. Anger jumped out from his eyebrow and Greed from his lips. Vak, the goddess of speech, appeared from his mouth. From his male parts emerged the oceans. Nirriti, the goddess of destruction, dropped out of his lower body. From Brahma's shadow came Rishi Kardama. All his creations appeared from his body and mind.

POPULAR BELIEFS

People born under this nakshatra have a tendency to get to the bottom or the root of things. They are independent and determined and won't rest until and unless they have exhausted all the weapons in their armoury to get to their goals. These attributes remind one of Nirriti – she is determined to achieve her goals and has an independent streak.

It is believed that by worshipping Nirriti with a sincere and pure devotion, one's sorrows will decrease and sins will be reduced. There is indeed a silver lining in the dark clouds following Nirriti.

20

PURVA ASHADHA NAKSHATRA

Deity: Apah,
Super-Mom of the Cosmic World

Purva Ashadha, the twentieth nakshatra, has a fabulous meaning – 'former invincible one' or 'former unconquered.' Imagine being considered invincible or unconquered. Its second name 'Aparajita' too has a wonderful meaning. Undefeated. It is a description that will definitely find lots of appeal.

This nakshatra is represented in the sky by three bright stars: Epsilon Sagittarii, Delta Sagittarii, and Lambda Sagittarii in the Sagittarius constellation. Epsilon Sagittarii is the brightest of the lot. It is also known as Kaus Australis. Delta and Lambda Sagittarii are called Kaus Media and Kaus Borealis, respectively. This trio of stars forms a gentle arc or curve. As the Milky way passes through this constellation, these stars are relatively easy to locate.

Now, our ancient seers had no interest in simple explanations. So, when they saw the shape this trio of stars made, they quickly ascribed the symbol of a handheld fan to this nakshatra. The second symbol is that of a winnowing basket used for ridding grains of husks. The third symbol is an elephant tusk. All these symbols have no similarity whatsoever.

Venus (Shukra) is the ruling planet of this nakshatra. It is the hottest planet in the solar system.

Rishi Pulaha is connected with Purva Ashadha nakshatra. His immense devotion to Lord Shiva pleased the lord, and he manifested as a Shivalinga in Varanasi.

This Shivalinga is called Pulaheshwar, a testimony to the devotion of this rishi.

The deity presiding over this nakshatra is goddess Apah. In Sanskrit, *apa* or *apas* translates as water. In the Rig Veda, Apah is deified as goddess of cosmic water. She is gentle, yet powerful. She not only nurtures, cleanses, and purifies her devotees, but also blesses them with strength and immortality. Her short and sweet name has a musical cadence to it, as it literally holds an ocean in its womb.

The ancient seers, recognizing the role of water as one of the life-sustaining forces in the universe, glorified it and bestowed on it the status of a female deity, crediting her with the powers of nourishing, healing, purifying, and also fulfilling desires. The water goddess juggled with so many responsibilities, like a super mom – looking after devotees and blessing them with all kinds of boons, participating in yagnas when sincerely invoked by her devotees, taking a small part of the offerings made to her and, in return, showering her choicest blessings on their devotees.

Many hymns in the Rig Veda are dedicated to the waters. It has another term for the waters – Salilam or Salila. Water was the first stage of creation and from this cosmic water emerged all life. The original substance of life is water say the hymns in the Satapatha Brahmana (a commentary on the Sukla Yajurveda) (IV.1.3).

Apah figured in the daily prayers called the Sandhya Vandana of the people of olden times.

Apo hista mayobhuvahsta na urje dadhatana
Mahe-ranaya caksase
Yo vah sivatamo rasastasya bhajayateha nah
Usatiriva matarah

Meaning: O water, the source of all happiness, the affectionate and loving Mother, please grant us energy-giving food, and an insight and wisdom to enjoy your divine splendour.

But, Apah could also refer to all the river goddesses. We just don't think of rivers as sources of water, we worship them as goddesses, considering them as mother goddesses. Riversides are where we perform important rituals. Let's delve a bit more into these super-moms aka rivers.

The most sacred river is Ganga or Ganges, people call her Ma Ganga. A revered goddess, she is depicted as flowing out of Shiva's matted locks. She was brought down to earth for a specific purpose, that of providing salvation to humankind. A dip in her sacred waters purifies the devotees, freeing them from sins. It is for this reason that she is called Mokshdayini.

Close behind the Ganges is the Yamuna River, descending from the Yamunotri glacier of Uttarakhand. This sacred river is the daughter of Surya and Sanjana.

Another revered river is the Narmada. Its origin is attributed to Shiva. One day when Shiva was meditating, the heat of his tapasya made the god sweat. The droplets started collecting (some legends say it was a tank in which this perspiration started dropping). Shiva continued his meditation, his sweating intensified and the sweat in the tank overflowed. This formed the river Narmada. It originates from Amarkantak on the hill by the same name in Madhya Pradesh.

The river Kaveri, too, enjoys a hallowed status, worshipped by many. Originating from the Talakaveri region in the Brahmagiri range of the Western Ghats in the Kodagu district of Karnataka, Kaveri is worshipped by the people of Karnataka and Tamil Nadu as it flows through these two states. Considered as Goddess Kaveriamma or Kaveri Amman, she has an unusual story attributed to her origin. A long, long time back there was a king named Kavera. With Brahma's blessings, he and his wife had a daughter who they named Kaveri. When Kaveri grew up, she was married to Rishi Agastya. Now there is a quaint story, associated with her origin as a river. According to the story when Agastya went for his bath, he wanted to safeguard his wife, so he turned her into water in his kamandalu. But sadly, the moment his back was turned, Ganesha who had taken the form of a crow accidentally overturned the kamandalu and all the water inside it flowed out in the form of the river Kaveri. Kaveri is known as Ganges of the South or Dakshina Ganga.

Godavari, which starts in Maharashtra, also has a unique story attributed to its origin. The famous Rishi Gautama and his wife Ahalya lived in the Brahmagiri Hills at Trimbakeshwar. For their daily food needs, they had a small stock of rice in their hermitage. But one day a hungry cow (some stories believe that it wasn't a real cow but an illusion created by a few sages who had sought refuge in

Gautama rishi's ashram during a famine and now wanted to leave the hermitage using the cow as an excuse) entered the hut where the rice was stored and started eating the rice. Gautama wanted to keep the rice safe, so he tried to push the cow away from his stock of rice by trying to scare the animal with the durbha grass which was found in abundance in his hermitage. But as the cow (illusion) was weak, it fell on the ground and died. Gautama was saddened and also alarmed as it was tantamount to 'Gohatya,' the killing of a cow, an animal considered sacred by Hindus. Gautama, through his powers, realized that the sages had deceived him. He cursed the sages, yet he decided to atone for the sin he had committed, albeit accidentally and unintentionally. He started praying to Shiva. The prayer wasn't asking the god to pardon him for this sin, but was a request to the god to divert the flow of the Ganga so that he could purify himself and his hermitage in its holy waters. So intense was Gautama's tapasya, that it pleased Shiva and he appeared before the rishi. The kind god diverted the river Ganga so that it flowed outside Gautama's hermitage. Gautama immediately took a dip in the river to purify himself of the sin he had committed.

Shiva poured the water from his own kamandalu over the dead cow. It instantly came back to life. The water from Shiva's waterpot created the river Godavari. Gautama was not just relieved of his sin, he also ended up being responsible for bringing the river Ganga to Trimbakeshwar. The locals call the Godavari river Gautami to honour the rishi who was instrumental in bringing the river there.

The water goddesses are treated with reverence. In the Atharvaveda, Apah is given importance and is also considered the mother of the entire universe with seven hymns dedicated to her. As a mother, she looks after her offsprings (the people) blessing them in innumerable ways.

POPULAR BELIEFS

People born under this nakshatra are hardworking and always motivated to strive for success. Ambition and bravery are a part of their nature. They can be both gentle and intense, just like water, the physical manifestation of Apah.

None of us can imagine a life without water. Water can purify and nourish. It can be harsh too, when there are floods that wreak havoc on both man and beast, plant and nature. Water was there when the universe started, it will be there when it ends.

21

UTTARA ASHADHA NAKSHATRA

Deity: Ten Vishvadevas, *The Guardians of Goodness*

The name of the twenty-first nakshatra Uttara Ashadha makes one realize that it may be forming a pair with Purva Ashadha. Both have a similar-sounding name, like a pair of twins. Uttara Ashadha means 'latter invincible one' or 'latter unconquered.' The meanings give a sense of triumph, strength, and victory. A feeling that we are encountering something or someone who is invincible.

Four bright stars in the Sagittarius constellation represent this nakshatra in the sky: Sigma Sagittarii (Nunki), Tau Sagittarii, Phi Sagittarii, and Zeta Sagittarii (Ascella). They occupy the last portion of this constellation. It is really not

surprising that the Vedic seers of olden times saw the shape of an elephant's tusk when they watched and studied these stars. An elephant's tusk is a symbol of its power and also beauty. A tusk may also decide whether the elephant is suitable for a leadership role.

Purva Ashadha and Uttara Ashadha are like two close companions. Just as they come one after the other in the sky, they also share a special symbol – the strong, lustrous tusk of an elephant. During ancient times, kings rode on elephants; elephants were a part of royal processions and even wars. Indra's majestic elephant Airavata is as popular as the god himself.

Venus (Shukra) is the ruling planet of this nakshatra. It is the second-brightest object in the night sky owing to the planet's clouds that are made of sulphuric acid droplets, which are highly reflective. The atmospheric pressure on Venus is around ninety-two times more than that of Earth's. That's a lot.

Rishi Kratu is associated with this nakshatra. Kratu's name in Sanskrit means 'sacrifice' or 'offering.' He was a devotee of Vishnu and through his intense tapasya pleased the preserver and attained great powers.

This nakshatra has not one but ten ruling deities. They are the ten Vishvadevas. *Vishva* means 'entire universe' and deva means 'god.' Vishvadevas translates to 'universal gods.' These Vedic gods are guardians of goodness. Their names are: Vasu (goodness), Satya (truth), Daksha (ritual skill), Kala (time), Kama (desire/lust), Kratu (willpower), Dhriti (firmness/forbearance), Pururavas (brightness/abundance), Madravas (peak of joy), and Kuru (ancestors). So, if you want people to be good to you, then it is these ten young and handsome gods you must pray to.

Fiercely protective of their devotees, these gods safeguard them by vanquishing their enemies. They can be easily won over with devotion and sincere prayers and as a reward they grant their devotees a whole lot of wishes in this world and an auspicious abode in the afterlife. That's so wonderful. Protection plus a great afterlife – a win-win situation.

Not everyone knew about the Vishvadevas. The Vishnu Purana and Vayu Purana refer to them as the sons of Vishva and Dharma. Vishva was one of the daughters of Prajapati Daksha; she was married to Dharmadeva. Just like the Moon god had married Daksha's twenty-seven daughters (nakshatras), Dharmadeva had married his other ten daughters.

There is a beautiful story in the Rig Veda about the Vishvadevas and Agni. One day, Agni saw his three older brothers carrying the offerings of the yagnas to the respective devas. Sadly, Agni's three brothers all died as they were unable to withstand the vashatkaras – the sound of vashat that is chanted in yagnas, just like the swahakaras and the omkaras (the sounds of swaha and om). Agni was scared that he, too, would end up dead due to the harsh sounds. So, he sought the sanctity of the celestial waters and hid himself to avoid being a part of the yagna that had claimed his siblings' lives.

A yagna is impossible without Agni, the sacred fire. The Vishvadevas were sent in search of him. They spread themselves far and wide to look for the Fire god. On finding him, they coaxed him to return to the yagna so it could continue and Agni could take the offering of the yagnas to the gods. What do you think clever Agni asked for? Not noise-cancelling headphones. Nor was it a fire-proof armour. It wasn't a heat-proof mask either. A smart god, Agni added a clause. He asked the gods that he be given importance both during the main part of the yagna as well as the second part, that he should get both the primary as well as the secondary offering. The Vishvadevas agreed as they had to get Agni back to the yagna any which way. And Agni got what he wanted.

When the Vishvadevas aren't helping the gods or doing their deity duties, they are engaged in their tapasya as they are tapasvis. They had performed intense penance in the Himalayas to the pitrs. This act of devotion pleased Brahma and, as was his custom, the creator granted them a boon. It wasn't some superpower like the asuras usually asked for. As a reward for their devotion and prayers to the pitrs, Brahma ensured that they would get a part of the shraddha offerings (the offering to the ancestors). The creator didn't just stop there; he also said that they would be honoured first during the shraddha ritual. That's a great boon to receive.

Thanks to Brahma's boon, the Vishvadevas hold a lot of importance during rituals and are supposed to have a liking for daily offerings according to the Manusmriti. Omniscient, omnipotent, and omnipresent, while these gods of the universe reside in heaven, they come down to earth when a sincere offering is made to them and fulfil the wishes of their devotees.

Around fifty-eight *suktas* or hymns are dedicated to the Vishvadevas in the Rig Veda. No one knows the exact number of these gods. Some texts mention ten, some say they're thirty-three (with eleven in heaven, eleven in space, and eleven on earth), others (Rig Veda specifically) attribute the number 3,339 to them. That's a mind-boggling number.

Vishvadevas are protectors of Rta. They went on a creation spree and created the directions and the seasons. Most of the gods are big-time multitaskers. Time management is their forte. And they have several skills up their sleeves.

Hope you all remember Vishwamitra? We discussed him in detail in one of the earlier chapters. Another story mentions that five of the Vishvadevas were cursed by Vishwamitra to be born on earth when they intervened between Vishwamitra and King Harishchandra. They incarnated as the Upapandavas, the five sons of Draupadi with the Pandavas. After they were killed in the Kurukshetra War at night by Ashwatthama, who mistook them to be the five Pandavas, they returned to heaven in their original form as the Vishvadevas. They must have breathed a sigh of relief to return to heaven.

POPULAR BELIEFS

People born under this nakshatra are intelligent, ambitious, positive, and introspective, just like the guardians of goodness. They respect traditions and values and believe in adhering to them, again this aspect reminds one of the Vishvadevas. They also give good advice. So, if you are seeking some solid advice, look no further.

It is due to these gods guarding goodness and protecting the order in the universe that chaos is minimized. These guardians of goodness sure are an asset to the world.

22

SHRAVANA NAKSHATRA

Deity: Vishnu, *The Vamana Avatar*

Shravana, the twenty-second nakshatra, also shares its name with Shravana month, which is the fifth month of the Hindu lunar calendar. It is considered a very sacred month. *Shrava* means 'ear,' 'hearing,' or 'one who limps.' The idea of limping or uneven steps finds an association with the three steps Vamana, the fifth avatar of Vishnu, took to reclaim the three worlds from Bali, the powerful asura king. Vishnu is also known as Trivikrama, which means three steps. The nakshatra has another name – 'Ashvattha,' which means the sacred Peepal tree, also known as *Ficus religiosa*.

This nakshatra is represented by three bright stars huddled together in the Aquila constellation: Alpha Aquilae, also known as Altair; Beta Aquilae, also known as Alshain; and Gamma Aquilae, also known as Tarazed. Altair's brightness makes it easily visible in the dark skies.

Apart from the three uneven steps, another symbol of this nakshatra is an ear.

The ear symbolizes listening, which is the first step in learning, imbibing, and eventually applying whatever one has learnt to one's daily life. In the olden times, there were no textbooks. Whatever the guru or teacher taught was transmitted orally to the shishya. They had to possess the keenness to listen and the ability to assimilate the guru's words. Knowledge of the Vedas has reached us only through Shruti, which means 'that which is heard.' This knowledge of the Vedas was passed down orally from the rishis and gurus to the disciple. This listening can also have another meaning. We all have an inner voice, the voice of our conscience, of our intuition. We can use this voice as our guide when we are confused in life or when we are at crossroads. When the disciple hears the Upanishads from the guru, it is called Shravana. The disciple has to think and introspect on the words of his guru.

Moon (Chandra) is the ruling planet of this nakshatra. Monday is Chandra deva's, or the Moon god's, day. Chandra deva is also known as Soma in Sanskrit and Monday is called Somavara. See the connection! Even in other cultures this association remains. In French, Monday is known as *Lundi* (*Lune* means moon). In Spanish, Monday is *Lunes* (*Luna* means moon). In German, Monday is *Montag* (*Mond* means moon).

Vashishta is the rishi associated with this nakshatra. He is one of the oldest Vedic sages. Vashishta was highly influential as kings and gods thronged to him for advice.

Vishnu is the deity of this nakshatra. In his Vamana avatar as a dwarf Brahmin boy, Vishnu teaches us never to judge a person by their outer appearance and built. Sometimes, even a dwarf can rise with great strength and stand firm against a giant. Vamana was Vishnu's fifth incarnation and the first in a fully human form. The first four were Matsya (the fish), Kurma (the tortoise), Varaha (the boar), and Narasimha (half man, half lion).

Vamana incarnated with the purpose of defeating the famous and powerful asura emperor Bali, the grandson of Prahlada. Prahlada, though an asura, was a renowned devotee of Vishnu. During this era, when Vamana incarnated as Vishnu, there was a constant war between the devas and the asuras. Bali had defeated Indra, the king of the devas, and captured all the three realms – heaven, earth, and the netherworld – disturbing the cosmic balance. Devas, the residents of heaven, were upset at their defeat. As usual, they rushed to Lord Vishnu's abode, pleading with him to get their kingdom back from the asura king.

Vishnu, always ready to help his devotees, assured them that he would reclaim heaven back for the devas. He took birth as Vamana, the son of mother goddess Aditi and sage Kashyapa. (We have already learnt how Aditi had prayed for a son who would defeat the powerful asura.)

Bali was conducting a yagna in gratitude for his conquests and for becoming the supreme ruler of all the three realms.

The large-hearted emperor announced that he would give anything a person asked of him during the yagna.

Vamana reached the place where the yagna was being held, carrying a kamandalu and a wooden umbrella in his hands. Bali asked Vamana what he wanted. Vamana requested Bali for just enough land that he could cover in three steps. Bali was thrilled at this modest request as it wouldn't make a hole in his treasury. This small brahmin could have asked for gold, silver, cows, grains, anything, but he had asked for just enough land that he could cover in three steps. And as he was so short, his three steps would be so tiny, not even enough to make an anthill.

Bali's guru, Shukracharya, who stood beside him, sensed something amiss and warned him. Shukracharya was the guru of the asuras, teaching them about war and weapons, politics, and other skills that gave the demons their power.

But Bali was in no mood to listen. He was honour-bound to fulfil his vow and accede to the brahmin boy's request.

Vamana tilted his water pot to pour some water into Bali's palms, as was the custom. Bali had to make a *sankalpa* (vow) before granting the brahmin boy's request. At this exact moment, Shukracharya recognized that Vamana was none other than Lord Vishnu.

The guru had to do something fast. To protect his disciple, he shrank to a tiny form and blocked the spout, preventing the water from flowing so the ritual wouldn't be complete. Vamana, the all-knowing Vishnu, recognized this trick. To clear the blockage, he inserted a sharp blade of grass into the spout. The grass pierced one of the eyes of Shukracharya, making him blind in one eye.

With Shukracharya distracted by his pain, the ritual was complete. After Bali drank the sanctified water Vamana poured into his palm, he decided it was time to show his true size. He grew taller and taller, until his head disappeared into the clouds. This was his gigantic Trivikrama form.

Shukracharya was also skilled in Sanjeevani Vidya (he had undertaken severe austerities to get this powerful boon from Shiva), a treatise that was full of knowledge to bring the dead back to life. With this powerful Sanjeevani mantra that revived dead people, he could revive the dead asuras back to life so they could resume their fights with the devas. His counterpart Brihaspati, who was the guru of the devas, didn't possess this vital knowledge. Shukracharya felt that Vamana wasn't the innocent dwarf brahmin he pretended to be. These rishis had sharp powers and could look through all kinds of disguises to know who the person standing before them was.

He took the first step and covered the entire earth. Bali watched wide-eyed as Vamana took the second step and covered the entire heaven. Now, as there was no place left for the third step, Vamana turned to Bali and asked him where he should place his third and last step.

Bali recognized the divinity in the brahmin boy. He was truly humbled. As he had given his word, he placed his head at Vamana's feet for him to take the last step.

Vamana placed his foot on Bali's head, and pushed him into Patala loka, the netherworld. Pleased with Bali's humility and sincerity in keeping his promise, Vishnu made him the king of the netherworld and blessed him with immortality. He also gave him permission to return to earth once a year, for ten days, to meet the people he had ruled over. This is the symbolism of the Onam festival, the return of Bali to earth. Vishnu also gave Bali a boon. He could ask for anything. Bali requested Vishnu to guard his palace. Vishnu readily agreed.

Now, as Bali wasn't around, the asuras lost their power and were soon vanquished by the devas and Indra got back his kingdom. Though it was a win-win situation for the devas, Goddess Lakshmi was unhappy as her husband Vishnu was spending all his time guarding Bali's palace. Lakshmi arrived at Bali's palace and tied a rakhi on his wrist. Now Bali was bound by the sacred thread and had to give his new sister a gift. Lakshmi asked Bali to release her husband so that he could return with her to his abode, Vaikuntha. Bali couldn't refuse. He allowed Vishnu to return to his abode. This is also symbolic of the festival of Raksha Bandhan.

POPULAR BELIEFS

People born under this nakshatra are known for their amicable nature and prefer to have a peaceful equation with everyone. Perseverance and commitment are qualities that make them reliable – they seldom leave things halfway, preferring to complete all the tasks and endeavours they have undertaken, just like Vamana, who preferred to complete his mission of ousting Bali.

The Vamana avatar shows that smartness can come in a small package. That one's true strength lies in one's quick-thinking and ingenuity.

23

DHANISHTA NAKSHATRA

Deity: Vasus, A *Harsh Curse*

Dhanishta is the twenty-third nakshatra. The name means 'wealthiest' or 'most beneficent.' Dhanishta has another name – Shravishta, which means 'most famous' or 'most heard of.' All the four meanings signify this nakshatra's association with abundance and good luck.

The name Shravishta has another explanation. Before Dhanishta is the Shravana nakshatra. Combine the first part of Shravana with the last part of Dhanishta and we get a cool new name, Shravishta, carrying with it an aura of luck and a halo of wealth. This also shows that both these nakshatras form a pair.

Four stars, namely Alpha Delphini (Sualocin), Beta Delphini (Rotanev), Delta Delphini, and Gamma Delphini, represent this nakshatra in the sky. They lie in the Delphinus constellation. Delphinus means 'dolphin' in Latin. Beta

Delphini is the brightest in the constellation. These stars form the shape of a rhombus, which according to the ancients resembles a musical drum. Though most seers and scholars differ on what type of drum it is, popular opinion refers to it as *damru* or *damaru*, Lord Shiva's favourite musical instrument.

Damru, the hourglass-shaped drum, is associated with Shiva, especially his cosmic dancer form Nataraja that performs the Tandava. The sound of the damru is symbolic of the pulse of the universe and represents the cosmic sound. It shows Shiva's power to control the forces of nature, however strong or big they may be.

In many images of Shiva, though he isn't holding the damru, it is tied to his *trishul* (trident). There is a belief that when Shiva played the damru, the first sound called 'nada' was produced in the universe. And Shiva started his cosmic dance of creation to the rhythm of the damru. From his dance, the world was born.

There is profound symbolism attached to the unique shape of the damru. One part depicts the Purusha, the male's part in procreation, and the other part represents Prakriti, the female's part in procreation. The union of these two forces symbolized by the *lingam* and the *yoni* results in *srushti* or creation. It also gave rise to *chaitanyam* (movement), *vac* (speech), and *shabda* (sound).

The midsection of the damru represents the point of union. Destruction happens when these two sections separate from each other. The shape of the damru also points to the nature of the universe, the duality it encompasses and the way two opposites (male and female) unite to create another human.

The ruling planet of this nakshatra is Mars (Mangal). Mars takes nearly twice the time Earth takes to complete one full revolution around the Sun. The surface of Mars has a very low atmospheric pressure, this is the reason why water isn't able to exist on its surface for long.

The rishi associated with this nakshatra is Angiras. This revered rishi composed many hymns and mantras and is also considered a Prajapati by many.

Eight deities known as Vasus preside over this nakshatra. *Vasu* means 'superb,' 'excellent,' or 'wealthy.' From this group, one particular Vasu, Bhishma, is one of the most loved characters from the Mahabharata. We can call him everyone's favourite character.

The deities of earthly abundance and light, Vasus are associated with natural elements. Also considered elemental gods, they are believed to be attendants of Indra.

The Ramayana mentions them as sons of Rishi Kashyapa and Aditi, while the Mahabharata considers them sons of Manu or Brahma. The later texts consider the Vasus as demigods, all associated with Vishnu. For this reason, Vishnu is also called Vasubandhu (a relative or friend of Vasus).

The Vasus were born on earth due to a curse from Rishi Vashishta. Let's delve into their story. The Vasus were celestial beings living in heaven. One day when they were in the forest, enjoying the tranquillity of nature and its creatures, the wife of Prabhasa (Sky Vasu), saw the wish-fulfilling cow Kamadhenu and desired to possess it. Prabhasa took the help of his seven brothers to steal the cow. With his divine powers, Vashishta came to know that the one who had taken his cow was the Sky Vasu. The rishi was furious and cursed all the Vasus that as they were behaving like humans, they would all be born as humans on earth.

Everyone knew of the power of the rishi's words. The scared Vasus rushed to the rishi's hermitage and pleaded for mercy, begging him to remove the curse. Curses cannot be removed, they can only be tweaked.

Vashishta's heart softened at their plight. But the words of the curse had left his mouth never to return. He told the seven Vasus that their lives on earth would be very short so as to fulfil his curse, but the eighth Vasu who had actually stolen the cow, would have to bear the full brunt of the curse and would have to endure a long life, full of hardship. The eighth Vasu was heartbroken.

The concerned Vasus appealed to River Ganga to help them out of this predicament. She agreed to assist them by becoming their mother when they took birth on earth. They left, relieved with her promise that after they were born from her womb on earth, she would release them from the curse by immersing them in water. Transforming into a woman, she appeared before King Shantanu. The king fell in love with the beautiful Ganga and asked her to marry him. Ganga agreed to Shantanu's proposal on one condition, that whatever happened he would never question her actions.

According to the curse of the Vasus, every time Ganga gave birth to a child, she drowned the newborn son in the river. Though Shantanu was shocked and heartbroken, he didn't question her actions, as he didn't want her to leave him. This way Ganga drowned seven of her children as she had promised the Vasus, freeing them from their misery.

But when Ganga planned to drown her eighth child – Prabhasa, the Sky Vasu – a distraught Shantanu couldn't control himself and forgot the condition he had agreed upon before Ganga married him. He begged her not to drown her son, but to spare him. Bound by her promise that she would leave him the moment he questioned her, Ganga assumed her original form and departed, leaving the young baby, a son named Devarata, in Shantanu's care.

Devarata grew into a young man whose life was dedicated to serving both his father, Shantanu, and the Kuru dynasty. To appease his father's wife, he took a lifelong oath of celibacy so that his children wouldn't stake a claim to the throne. This oath gave him the title of Bhishma, 'the great one or the one with the great (terrible) oath.' His vow sent fears of apprehension down peoples' spines.

Bhishma's life was a series of selfless acts and sacrifices for his father, family, and the kingdom that he guided and the subsequent kings he mentored. His end on a bed of arrows from Arjuna's bow, during the last few days of the Kurukshetra War, was both painful and stretched out, a result of the curse that his life fulfilled.

Bhishma was a prince of the Kuru kingdom. He was the commander of the Kauravas' army during the war fought between the Kauravas and the Pandavas. Bhishma was also known as Gangaputra, Devarata, and Pitamaha, and had a life filled with hardship. A life that a lesser mortal wouldn't have been able to endure. He witnessed his clan, the Kauravas and the Pandavas, fighting at the Kurukshetra War, or the Mahabharata War, and the death of loved ones. The curse of Vashishta wasn't easy to endure. But Bhishma endured everything with a calm acceptance of his fate.

POPULAR BELIEFS

People born under this nakshatra have the ability to adapt to any situation they are put in, just like Bhishma had the flexibility to mould himself to different situations and emerge victorious. They also make excellent conversationalists, one can chat with them till the wee hours of the morning. They also have this innate ability to put others at ease instantly and make them comfortable. So, they are great to be around with.

Bhishma was a man of his words. Once he promised something, he ensured that he would fulfil his oath, come what may. His oath became a gigantic wall that nothing could pull down. To keep our promises is an admirable virtue that is a good habit to cultivate.

24

SHATABHISHA NAKSHATRA

Deity: Varuna, *The One Who Travels on the Crocodile Vahana*

Whether one spells it as 'Shatabhisha' or 'Shatabhishak,' the meaning of this twenty-fourth nakshatra remains the same. Both translate as 'hundred physicians,' 'hundred medicines,' 'possessing a hundred healers,' or 'hundred flowers.' This nakshatra has another name – Shatataraka, implying 'possessing a hundred stars.'

A group of faint stars in the centre of the Aquarius constellation represents this nakshatra. Gamma Aquarii, or Sadachbia, is the brightest among them. An empty circle is the main symbol of this nakshatra. A circle is never ending, with no noticeable beginning or end. The circle of life, the circle of seasons, the circle of protection. Circles are mysterious and full of secrets. Perhaps they imbue the people born under this star with a secret nature. An empty circle also denotes that all creation rose out of nothingness and will dissolve into nothingness.

Rahu (North Lunar Node) is the ruling planet of this nakshatra. It is the eighth graha of the nine navagrahas. Hindu astronomy attributes this shadow planet as the cause of the solar eclipse when Rahu covers the Sun.

Atri is the rishi associated with this nakshatra. It is said that Atri and his wife, Anusuya, had the honour and privilege of welcoming Rama, Sita, and Lakshmana in their hermitage in Chitrakoot when the three were exiled for fourteen years.

Though there are hundred physicians associated with this nakshatra, there is just one deity presiding it: Varuna, the god of water and cosmic order. He is one of the earliest deities in the Hindu pantheon, and it is believed that his initial association was with the sky. Varuna is symbolic of the setting sun. This deity has two BFF's – Aryaman and Mitra (his siblings are also his good friends). Whenever the two are mentioned, Varuna's name always comes up in some or the other way.

Varuna is depicted riding his vahana Makara, a mythical creature who is commonly portrayed as a crocodile. He holds a pot in one hand and carries a *pasha* (a noose) in the other.

One of Varuna's duties is to be the guardian of Rta, the ethical, moral, social, and religious laws that bind man to the right path, the path of dharma. Due to this designation,

Varuna is a bit strict. Just like the way the principal of the school has to be strict. Else the students will be unruly. If anyone steps even a little out of that path, then nothing can save them from Varuna's noose with its three folds.

Varuna had a strong grip on Maya (the mystic powers) and he watches the world with his keen eyes, like the tough invigilator who ensures no student is pulling out slips of papers with the answers written, in the exam hall. Varuna also had spies working for him, so that he can punish the ones who erred. This sounds scary as one never knows who the spies are. It could be the man sitting next to you on the train when you are sticking chewing gum on the seat or the bird watching you throw stuff from a window.

If one were to go by the Rig Veda, especially the initial part, Varuna gets a bit of a fearful image as he was considered the guardian or the upholder of moral law, meting out punishment to the sinners. But this had a clause, those who sinned and were unrepentant about it were punished, and those who sinned and repented were forgiven. Many hymns of the Rig Veda praise his association with water and water bodies.

The handsome Varuna has his abode under the waters (Samudra) in a palace with huge pillars and columns, with the god sitting on a resplendent throne with his wife, Varuni, by his side. Both husband and wife wear shiny robes, silken garments, and glittering jewels, looking as radiant as the sun. The view from Varuna's palace is the stuff of dreams, surrounded as it is by aquatic creatures, nagas, and flowing waters. Varuna doesn't have time to enjoy his waterside property as he is an extremely busy god, juggling so many responsibilities – one of his jobs is to ensure timely and plentiful rains and he does this dutifully, year after year. Varuni represents the intoxicating qualities of water, the power it wields over man, plants, and other creatures.

An interesting point to note is that during the Vedic times, Varuna was almost always invoked with Mitra during yagnas, as though they were two bodies in one soul. Both were invited to sit on the northern (north is the side of the gods) side of the yagna. They were beseeched to bring good rains that would result in a bountiful harvest. They were also requested to protect the Rta. Varuna ensured that yagnas were conducted properly, he also made sure that negative influences that could disrupt the yagnas were kept at bay, ushering positive influences so the effect of the ritual was maximized. He guarded *satya* (truth) and stood against *an-rta* (lies). But post the Vedic times, this hallowed seat was taken away from Varuna and Mitra, and they were moved to the west, a direction that didn't have much clout or wield any kind of power. Later, Varuna was considered a dikpala, a guardian of the west direction and he became symbolic of the setting sun.

What many don't know is that Varuna was also a wise seer. He taught his son Bhrigu all the secrets of Brahman. It would be nice to have such a guru, one who can teach us all the difficult-to-understand stuff in a simple and easy-to-learn style.

In spite of all his wisdom, it wasn't all smooth sailing for Varuna. He once earned the anger of Lord Rama. When Rama and the monkey army were waiting at the shores to cross the ocean to reach Lanka and save Sita, the waters were in a turbulent mood and they were unable to cross it. Rama and the army waited for three days and nights. When the tides still didn't subside, Rama became angry and readied his powerful weapon, the dreaded Brahmastra, and warned the Samudra deva of its repercussions – it would dry up the ocean and destroy all the creatures of the water. Varuna became frightened and emerged from the waters, his palms joined in repentance. He pleaded with Rama to calm down and have mercy on him. As the sea calmed down, its waves subsided and Rama's army was able to build a bridge made of stones over it and they eventually reached the island of Lanka.

There are not many temples featuring Varuna. Bundi in Rajasthan holds the distinction of having a famous shrine of Varuna. In the Nawal Sagar Lake, a square-shaped artificial lake, is the partially submerged temple of Varuna.

According to the Brihadaranyaka Upanishad, water alone existed in the beginning. From water came satya (truth). From satya emerged Brahman. From Brahman, the Prajapatis were born. These Prajapatis produced all the gods. And all these gods worship only the truth.

After the Vedic times, Varuna, along with Indra, lost his power and prestige, and he was relegated to a minor role in the vast pantheon of gods.

Let us learn a Varuna Mantra:

Aum Jalbimbaye Vidmahe
Nila Purushaye Dhimaahi
Tanno Varunah Prachodayat

Meaning:

Aum, let us pray and meditate on the water and its reflection. O god of the blue ocean, bestow on me a higher intellect. May the god of water grant me intellect and illumination of my mind.

POPULAR BELIEFS

People born under this nakshatra are constantly on guard due to their suspicious nature. This is so reminiscent of Varuna; he, too, had to be on constant vigil due to his responsibility of guarding Rta, the moral code or laws. They are also introverted by nature, preferring to go the reclusive way. They also love their own company more than anything else. They contemplate and get to the root of all problems.

Though Varuna was a god worshipped by many people, even he was scared of facing Rama's wrath. Goes to show that even the gods feared the other gods and their anger, as power didn't make them immune to curses or punishments.

25

PURVA BHADRAPADA NAKSHATRA

Deity: Aja Ekapada, *The Mysterious One-Footed God*

The name Purva Bhadrapada is a bit of a mouthful, but once you get the hang of it, the words flow out of your mouth. The alternative name of the twenty-fifth nakshatra is 'Purvaproshthapada.' *Purva Bhadrapada* means 'former (one who possesses) lucky feet.' *Purvaproshthapada* in turn means 'former (one who possesses) feet of a stool.' Both these literal translations of the words sound a bit odd. The meaning will become clear as we delve deeper.

Purva Bhadrapada is represented by two bright stars in the Pegasus constellation called Alpha Pegasi and Beta Pegasi. Both these stars can be easily spotted in the night sky. Alpha Pegasi is also known as Markab and Beta Pegasi as Scheat. When the ancient sages saw these two stars, they felt the stars represented the front legs of a bed or a funeral cot. Perhaps, the Great Square of Pegasus (formed by the stars Markab and Scheat of this nakshatra and Algenib and Alpheratz of the Uttara Bhadrapada nakshatra) must have appeared to them as a funeral cot.

The front legs of a funeral cot became the nakshatra's main symbol. Funeral cots signify our exit from the physical world. Another symbol is a man with two faces: one calm and the other angry or violent. The calm face is the one the world sees and the raging one is the private one, showing the individual's darker side. There is a third symbol - a sword, representing intellect. It also has a fourth symbol, a single ray of the sun.

Jupiter (Brihaspati) is the ruling planet of this nakshatra. It takes nearly twelve Earth years (11.86 Earth years to be exact) to complete one orbit around the Sun. But when it comes to rotating on its axis, as mentioned earlier, it can give Earth a run for its money as it takes just under ten hours to rotate on its axis.

Vashishta is the rishi associated with this nakshatra. Vashishta is believed to have lived near the banks of Ganga, somewhere in the present-day Uttarakhand. His wife, Arundhati, was well-known for her piousness and sometimes he was also called Arundhati Nath (husband of Arundhati).

Aja Ekapada (Ajikapada, Ajaikapada) is the presiding deity of Purva Bhadrapada nakshatra. Let's first understand the meaning of Aja Ekapada. If the words are broken into three parts, *Aja* means 'unborn' or 'uncreated,' *eka* means 'one,' and *pada* means 'foot.' *Aja Ekapada* translates to an 'unborn, single-footed one.' *Aja* in Sanskrit also means 'goat'; the name can be translated to 'one-footed goat.'

This Vedic deity is one-legged and dark. He is considered one of the Rudras (the fierce form of Shiva). Aja Ekapada is surrounded by ambiguity, so not much is known about

him or why Lord Shiva is depicted in this form but it is not worshipped by people unlike his other popular forms of Bhairava, Nataraja, Bholenath, and Shambu.

Aja Ekapada's origin is a huge conundrum. Certain Shaivite traditions and some tantric texts attribute Aja Ekapada's birth or origin to having manifested when Shiva was in his ascetic and cosmic form. Some people believe that Aja Ekapada, the one-legged god, appeared during Shiva's deep meditation. When Shiva sat still and was focusing deeply, the meditation generated a special energy and this energy gave birth to or turned into Aja Ekapada, the one-footed deity. Aja Ekapada's form is symbolic of Shiva's yogi form, someone who is so calm and peaceful, who needs nothing from the world and can easily transcend material existence to such an extent, that the entire cosmos watched him in awe. The trinity, especially Shiva and Vishnu, were known for their many avatars.

Aja Ekapada is considered a manifestation of Shiva's ascetic form. The energy of this deity is invoked during tantric rituals that are associated with cosmic energy and when the energy of the elemental forces needs to be tapped for a seeker's spiritual growth. Later texts consider Aja Ekapada as the lord of storms and destruction, which are attributes of Rudra. But in spite of all his associations, Aja Ekapada is representative of the balance that happens when chaos meets stability, when destruction approaches creation, and when ascetic detachment and materialism collide.

In some texts, there is mention of the Ekapada Bhairava form of Shiva, the one-legged or one-footed Shiva, and according to a few assumptions it has its origins in Aja Ekapada. Ekapada Bhairava finds a mention in many Agama texts. Agamas are a collection of Tantric literature. In Amsumadbhedagama, which is an Agamic text, he is described as wearing white silken clothes, with his matted hair piled on top of his head like a headdress, also called jata-mukuta. This three-eyed deity holds a trishul in one hand and a small hammer called a tanka in another. The remaining two hands form two mudras – Varada mudra, this is a boon-giving gesture, and the Abhaya mudra, a gesture of reassurance.

In another Agamic text called the Uttara-Karanagama, there is a mention of this Ekapada deity as Ekapada Trimurti. It is because a four-headed Brahma emerges from the right side of Ekapada and Vishnu emerges from his left side. The Ekapada Trimurti has the one-legged Shiva (Ekapada) standing tall on his single leg on the padma pitha (a lotus pedestal). This three-eyed and four-armed deity carries a tanka and a mriga in his two hands, the remaining two are in Varada and Abhaya mudras. The hairstyle is the same – jata-mukuta. As an extra embellishment, pearl earrings adorn Ekapada's ears. Here, the single foot of Ekapada is considered the axis mundi or the cosmic pillar of the universe. In this depiction, Shiva is the supreme lord from whom both Brahma and Vishnu emerge.

But for all the mystery surrounding his presence, this deity has been given an important task in the Atharva Veda. Aja Ekapada is referred to as the 'one who had stabilized both earth and heaven with his might.' This means that a single step of this unusual deity had brought stability in two different realms. The more we delve into Shiva's life, the more power we see in this god. Shiva has assumed different forms for different purposes, finishing the work other gods were unable to do, and then retreating to his abode Mount Kailash for his meditation.

The single leg of Aja Ekapada has plenty of symbolisms: it represents a balance between the physical and the spiritual world, it is symbolic of the cosmic pillar also known as the axis mundi – the cosmic or the mystical pillar of light that connects heaven to earth – and it also symbolizes ascetic detachment. Aja Ekapada's posture is representative of standing above the dualities of the world, with that single foot grounded or rooted in higher spiritual principles. If one were to give a simple explanation, we can define Aja Ekapada as the unborn cosmic energy that has a transcendent nature and is present in all humans. But it lies

There is a temple dedicated to the Ekapada Bhairava form of Shiva – it is called Ajaikapada Bhairava Temple. The temple is located in Jagatsinghpur district of Odisha. Ekapada statues can be found in many Shiva temples of south India. In certain parts of our country, Ekapada Bhairava is considered a tantric deity, as is Aja Ekapada.

unexplored. In the Vedas, Aja Ekapada was a revered deity and thought of as infinity.

Luckily for the gods, the many different forms of Shiva didn't go around handing out boons like the destroyer himself did. The reason for this was that the demons prayed more to Shiva than his other forms. Seeing all the asuras and their strange demands, Aja Ekapada must have made himself incognito and heaved a sigh of relief.

POPULAR BELIEFS

People born under this nakshatra are hardworking and sincere. They believe in taking the route of perseverance and give everything their very best, even when their goals are not big enough for others. Their commitment is unshaken, even if their results are not fruitful. Perseverance reminds one of Aja Ekapada, and the severe penance associated with this deity.

Aja Ekapada form of Shiva points to the fact that the gods, especially the Trinity, assumed different avatars or forms to fulfil a purpose and through these forms they also paid homage to the animals, considering these mute creatures an important part of nature.

26

UTTARA BHADRAPADA NAKSHATRA

Deity: Ahirbudhnya, *The Elusive One*

Uttara Bhadrapada nakshatra occupies the twenty-sixth position in the list of nakshatras. It follows the Purva Bhadrapada nakshatra. While *Purva Bhadrapada* means 'former lucky feet,' *Uttara Bhadrapada* means 'latter (one who possesses) lucky feet.' And just like its predecessor, it has an alias, an alternative name – 'Uttaraproshthapada,' meaning 'latter (one who possesses) feet of a stool.'

The two bright stars representing this nakshatra lie in two different constellations. In the Pegasus constellation lies the star Gamma Pegasi and in the Andromeda constellation lies the star Alpha Andromedae, which is also brighter than its companion. Actually, the entire Andromedae constellation is bright. Both these stars are easily visible in the night sky. Gamma Pegasi is also known as Algenib and Alpha Andromedae as Alpheratz.

When our ancient sages saw these stars, they somehow felt that it represented the back legs of a funeral cot, which became this nakshatra's symbol. Hope you remember the symbol of the previous nakshatra – the two front legs of a funeral cot. As mentioned earlier, the rectangular shape formed by the four stars of these nakshatras is also known as Great Square of Pegasus.

While the bed as a funeral cot is symbolic of a deep, eternal sleep from which there is no waking, this bed can also be seen as a sleeping bed – sleep is seen by many as a temporary form of death, where a person in unaware of the external world and sometimes visits a dream world.

Saturn (Shani) is the ruling planet of this nakshatra. This sixth planet from the Sun is named after the Roman god Saturnus. Saturn is the second largest planet in our solar system, a gas giant and it is also the flattest planet.

Pulaha is the rishi associated with this nakshatra. Renowned for his spiritual wisdom, Pulaha had started his austerities from a young age, as he wanted to reach the higher states of consciousness. As time passed, Pulaha's austerities grew in intensity.

Uttara Bhadrapada nakshatra's deity Ahirbudhnya is considered a mysterious figure. In Sanskrit, *ahi* means 'serpent' and *budhnya* means 'belonging to the depths.' Hence, his name means 'serpent of depths,' or a 'serpent that lies beneath the surface of the earth.' This water serpent can also be a dragon of the deep seas, who lives at the bottom of the ocean.

To meet this deity, you have to dive deep into the surface of the earth as well as the water. There is a reason this deity lives in such inaccessible places: he likes his privacy to such an extent that he prefers to live far away from everyone, seeking solitude and peace.

There isn't much written about this deity in Vedic texts, just a reference to him being a serpent god living in the depths of the earth, be it land or water, or even the netherworld. Considered as one of the eleven Rudras, this form of Shiva is considered benevolent and a wise teacher. Ahirbudhnya is also a lesser-known avatar of Shiva.

There are two stories about the birth of Ahirbudhnya. One story states that one day Brahma wanted to perform a yagna. All the preparations were done and the yagna started. After it was complete, Brahma in his prayers to the universe requested it to make the universe stable. He beseeched it to listen to his request and provide support. Brahma's prayers were answered by Shiva. Assuming the form of the yagna fire, Shiva incarnated as Ahirbudhnya. The Ahirbudhnya form of Shiva not only heard Brahma's request and prayers, but he also bestowed on him a boon: Brahma would be born in twelve forms. This dedication of Shiva's life force to Brahma, the creator, further ensured that Brahma could both protect his creation and also continue it. Ahirbudhnya's life was for the purpose of supporting creation.

Shiva's avatar of Ahirbudhnya has given rise to the term Rudra Sharpa, as Ahirbudhnya embodies the sacred essence of Rudra, as well as the energy of serpents. Through this Ahirbudhnya can also take the form of a serpent, though

he usually moves around as a sage or in an ascetic's disguise, sharing his profound spiritual wisdom and guiding spiritual aspirants on the path. Ahirbudhnya carries an aura of elusiveness and is an enigma, most don't know about him and even fewer have had the privilege of meeting him. And when this deity takes on the form of a serpent, it is a rare blessing indeed for the devotee to witness this blessed event.

There is a second version of Ahirbudhnya Rudra's birth. After Brahma had created the universe, he asked a boon from Shiva. The boon Brahma desired was that Shiva should incarnate in a form that was so unique that it would protect the universe. Shiva accepted the condition and granted Brahma the boon by manifesting in the Ahirbudhnya Rudra form, where Shiva joined forces with the serpents to safeguard the universe. That's why one of the translations of Ahirbudhnya's name is 'abode of snakes' or 'one who sits in the place of snakes.' We all know of Shiva's affiliation with snakes – he wears Vasuki around his neck.

Every deity has duties assigned to him or her. In the same way, this deity has been entrusted with the task of maintaining the fertility of the earth and keeping things in balance.

It is said that serpents exist in all planes. The Milky Way resembles a stream that can also be seen as a serpent meandering through the depths of the space or sky. Ahirbudhnya lives inside the celestial ocean and other snakes live in water and under the ground.

We also have serpents in our bodies. It is not the worms in our tummies that we are referring to. It is the Kundalini, the dormant spiritual energy represented by a coiled serpent at the base of the spine, in the Mooladhara (root) chakra. The Kundalini is the repository of the human's hitherto untapped spiritual energy that they are born with. Spiritual seekers try to awaken this sleeping kundalini, not with an alarm clock or shaking it to bring it out of its deep sleep, but with spiritual practices. When the kundalini is awakened through regular spiritual practices, which are done under the guidance of a guru or a teacher, this coiled serpent makes its way to the Sahasrara chakra on the crown of a human's head, leading to all kinds of spiritual siddhis, knowledge, and wisdom, elevating the ordinary human to a spiritual plane. This spiritual journey is always undertaken alone, away from the noisy world.

If we take another meaning of the word *ahirbudhnya* into consideration, it would represent our sub-conscious mind, with its connection to the universal consciousness and the power it contains, the infinite possibilities that it has the potential to lead us to.

Some consider Ahirbudhnya the king of the Nagas. A collection of writings on this mysterious deity can be found in the Ahirbudhnya Samhita. It is believed that when people worship Ahirbudhnya, this worship awakens their inner strength, provides spiritual protection as well as rids the devotee of their negative tendencies.

POPULAR BELIEFS

People born under this nakshatra are known for their determination to achieve their goals. This is so akin to Ahirbudhnya; he is so determined to achieve his goals that he retreats into solitude to achieve them. But this determination doesn't make them inflexible, rather it makes them adopt a flexible attitude so that their goals are met. They also have a strong sense of empathy and sympathy, which makes them more understanding.

Ahirbudhnya comes across as a kind and wise teacher, who will have all the answers, even the most difficult questions posed by the student/devotee will not go unanswered. He is a teacher who will walk alongside the student, guiding them all the way to their destination.

27

REVATI NAKSHATRA

Deity: Pushan,
The One Whose Teeth Were Smashed

Revati is the final, twenty-seventh nakshatra. Its name translates to 'wealthy.' There is another meaning of this nakshatra: 'to transcend.' This meaning is more apt as it goes with this nakshatra's final position.

Revati nakshatra is represented in the sky by Zeta Piscium, a multiple star system in the Pisces constellation. Though significant in Indian astronomy, it is faint and can be difficult to spot with the naked eye.

Our ancient seers saw the shape of a dhola, which is a drum with a strap, when they studied the pattern this cluster of stars formed. This drum is worn around one's neck and played with both hands, by hitting it with two sticks. This musical instrument accompanies joyous processions.

A drum is a symbol of this nakshatra. There is one more that of 'fish swimming in sea.' The symbolism of a fish shouldn't come as a surprise as this nakshatra is a part of Pisces constellation (two fish swimming in opposite directions represent this zodiac sign). The ancients used the example of a fish swimming in the sea as a symbol of a soul's passage in the waters of the universe. They saw the world (*sansar*) as a cosmic ocean.

The ruling planet of this nakshatra is Mercury (Budha), the smallest planet in the solar system. It is the second densest planet, after Earth. It will come as a surprise to you that Mercury has wrinkles. This is because the iron core of this planet has cooled and later contracted giving rise to wrinkles. These wrinkles are both high and long.

Kratu is the rishi associated with this nakshatra. This rishi's wisdom and knowledge made kings, sages, and those who were in search of the spiritual truths seek his company and learn from him, so that he could guide them and provide a solution to their problems.

The deity of this nakshatra is Pushan, a Vedic solar deity who lights up people's path. His name is derivative of the Sanskrit word *pushyati*, which means 'he nourishes' and 'makes people thrive.' In some texts, he is referred to as the nourisher. You get the connection between *pushan* and *poshan* (nourishing).

As the deity associated with a safe and secure travel, he illuminates travellers' paths (just like the sun) and offers them protection during their journey. This journey could also be the one from earth to heaven as Pushan is also familiar with the divine path that leads one to the afterlife. This gave him the title of a spirit guide, guiding the spirits of the departed from one world to the next.

The son of Rishi Kashyapa and Aditi, Pushan is one of the twelve Adityas. Just like every other Aditya, he assumes the role of the sun for a month every year and rules over the planet in that month. Riding in his chariot pulled by rams, he heralds the sun's arrival in the morning sky, just like his sibling Savitr does. In comparison to Surya, Pushan is gentler, has a nourishing quality, and bestows wealth and prosperity.

In the Vedas, Pushan is regarded as a guardian of herds and flocks. It is not just the humans he looked after, even animals like sheep, horses, and cattle come under his protective umbrella. Due to this he had another name – Pashupa, meaning 'protector of animals.' He is also granted the status of a deity who helps one recover animals and items lost, provides shelter, bestows fertility, and blesses one with abundance. So, if you ever lose important stuff, then Pushan can definitely help you find it. He is just a sincere prayer away.

Though Pushan is a multi-talented god and should have been the shining star of his family, standing under the spotlight, sadly his siblings stole his thunder and hogged all the limelight, getting the more glamorous job profiles and outshining their younger brother at everything. His brothers Indra and Surya were not just better known, in fact they were famous and took over his roles. As the sun nourished all the living beings on earth, Surya took over Pushan's role as the nourisher, and Indra, the god of rain and lightning, grabbed Pushan's role as the god of crops. Thus, both his brothers sidelined him and outshone him in every way. (Not sure if this celestial sibling rivalry led to fireworks at the family dining table and needed the intervention of the parents to settle arguments!)

Shiva's family also played a role in undermining Pushan, not deliberately but by accident. Ganesha took over Pushan's role as the god of journeys and as the remover of obstacles. As Shiva is also called Pashupati, the king of all animals, he managed to cast his large shadow over Pushan who was responsible for looking after the cattle.

Shiva has also been Pushan's nemesis in another way. After Shiva's wife, Sati, immolated herself during her father's yagna, Shiva's anguish and anger created a fierce creature known as Virabhadra who stormed towards the yagna site and started destroying Daksha's sacrifice.

Pushan was one of the deities invited for the grand yagna, a VIP guest. Pushan had been excited to be a special guest at the yagna. He was already visualizing his conversation with the Trinity (he had no idea that Shiva wasn't invited). He looked forward to chatting with the saptarishis and brushing shoulders with the other gods. He was sure the yagna would boast a mouth-watering spread. He had heard that preparations had started weeks back and many cooks had been hired.

Pushan arrived at the yagna, dressed in his special clothes, little knowing that the day wouldn't go well for him. Disaster never announces its arrival; it just pounces and devours the individual.

Some texts mention that an angry Shiva kicked Pushan when he was eating the offering. It is believed that the force of the kick was so powerful that it sent all of Pushan's teeth to outer space and these teeth are now stars in the Milky Way. The galaxy received additional stars, while the good-looking god with a pleasant face, braided hair, and a beard, ended up becoming toothless. This was the time before dentures had made their appearance. But for the gods, it would be easy to get a new set of teeth!

Puranic versions attribute Virabhadra to smashing Pushan's teeth. A heavy price to pay for a yagna invite. It is the sole reason this gentle god is stuck on a liquid diet preferring curd or food mashed to a pulp, which is easy to swallow, as an offering. Though later when things cooled down Shiva is supposed to have restored Pushan's teeth.

POPULAR BELIEFS

People born under this nakshatra are often dreamers, living in their own little fantasy worlds. Despite their dreamy nature, they are ever ready to help and support others. This aspect of their nature makes them appealing to others and they are well-liked by their circle of family and friends. Well, everyone likes a supportive person! This aspect of helping and supporting others also matches Pushan's nature, he got along well with the other deities and hardly had problems with anyone.

Pushan is also considered a kavi, a poet. So, if it is inspiration you are hoping for while writing essays, stories, and assignments, then Pushan can definitely help you. With Pushan's help, you will end up writing something that will wow the readers.

ABHIJIT

A Secret Nakshatra

The twenty-eighth nakshatra, going by the name of Abhijit, can become the subject of a great whodunnit or even a whydunnit? Is he (it is the only male nakshatra) or isn't he a nakshatra? If he is one, why is he the only male nakshatra, when the rest of the twenty-seven are female? If he is a nakshatra, then why is he not in the list of nakshatras?

Some believe that he is invisible, that's why he is missing from the list. Why does he wear an invisibility cloak? What makes him seek this solitude? What's his purpose? There are so many questions surrounding Abhijit nakshatra.

The literal meaning of *Abhijit* is 'undefeatable,' 'ever-conquering,' 'final victory,' or 'complete victory.' All these meanings point to just one description, that of triumph and achievement. Abhijit is complete dominance of good over everything else in the universe. It is probably the reason why the Bhagavad Gita mentions Lord Krishna saying: 'Amongst nakshatras, I am Abhijit.'

It is believed that this nakshatra is taken into consideration when the system of twenty-eight nakshatras is used. For the sake of making it easy, twenty-seven nakshatras are taken into consideration, as these twenty-seven have to be divided by nine grahas, hence each is assigned three nakshatras. But if twenty-eight were considered, then this calculation would go awry.

Whatever the reason for this nakshatra missing in action, Abhijit nakshatra is a big mystery that remains unsolved.

MEET THE OTHER STARS IN THE SKY

Dhruva Tara, *Immovable Boy*

Polaris, commonly called the North Star or the Pole Star, is a unique star lying in the Ursa Minor constellation. Its proximity to the rotational axis of the Earth, just above the North Pole (also known as the north celestial pole) makes it appear nearly stationary in the sky from the northern hemisphere.

The other stars surrounding it look as though they are rotating around it. This quality of Polaris star has made it a fixed point for scientists to take measurements and also to draw maps for both celestial navigation as well as for the purposes of astrometry. The Polaris is visible all through the year in the northern hemisphere.

The story of Dhruva (or Dhruv) Tara is one without which childhood storytelling sessions are incomplete. Dhruva's story is also a lesson in determination, perseverance, and faith. In Sanskrit, *dhruva* means 'unshakeable', or 'firm,' and this child devotee of Lord Vishnu proved that he was worthy of that title. It is no wonder then that he has been elevated to the status of the Pole Star, also known as Dhruvaloka, the abode of Lord Vishnu.

Before he became the Pole Star, Dhruva was just a young boy content with life and happy to play in his father's palace. His father, King Uttanapada, had two queens. His first wife was Suniti, a kind and gentle lady who gave birth to a boy named Dhruva, little did she know that he would take the family name to another level altogether, to the skies. The king's second wife was Suruchi. Her son was named Uttama.

As Dhruva was the eldest son, it would be his birthright to take over the kingdom after his father, as was the norm. But Suruchi had plans to make her son, Uttama, the king. For this reason, right from his childhood, she worked hard to make Uttama the king's favourite. One day, Dhruva, a child of five years, saw his younger brother sitting on the king's lap on the throne. Dhruva, too, wanted to sit on his father's lap. Suruchi, jealous of Dhruva, mocked him and told him that he should ask the gods for the blessing to be born from her womb, as that would grant him the privilege of sitting on the king's lap.

Dhruva's mother heard the conversation and consoled her sobbing son that this was his fate and he should accept it. But Dhruva was determined to hear about his fate from the lord's mouth, making a resolution to go in search of god. He set out on a journey to the forest.

The divine sage Narada, an ardent devotee of Vishnu, appeared before Dhruva and tried to dissuade him from his mission. But Dhruva was firm and not to be deterred from his chosen path. Seeing his determination, Narada guided the young boy, teaching him all the rituals and mantras he would need in his goal of seeking Lord Vishnu. It is believed that one of the mantras Narada taught Dhruva was *Om Namo Bhagvate Vasudevaya*. This Dwadasakshari mantra is a twelve-syllable mantra dedicated to Vishnu. Narada became the boy's guru and blessed him.

As advised by Narada, Dhruva started his meditation. The boy's penance worried Indra. He thought that Dhruva was after his throne. To break the boy's penance, Indra assumed the form of Dhruva's mother and requested him to return to the palace. But oblivious to this distraction, Dhruva continued meditating. Not accepting defeat, Indra sent snakes and monsters to disturb the boy. But Dhruva continued his meditation as though the reptiles and monsters didn't exist.

The boy's austerities increased. Initially, he ate only fruits, roots, and tuber. Next, he survived on dry leaves, then on water, and finally, he gave up everything, literally living on air. His penance was so severe, the young boy's concentration so focused and fierce, that his meditation shook the earth. The saptarishis meditating nearby were jolted out of their intense tapasya. They were astounded at the sight of the young boy, deeply absorbed in meditation. Surrounding him as a wall of protection, they started praying for him.

Finally, after many months, Vishnu appeared before Dhruva and granted him a wish. But by now Dhruva had overcome all his desires, forgotten the original reason for his penance. Now he had just one wish. To live a life in worship of Lord Vishnu. Initially rendered speechless by the vision of the lord, Dhruva later burst into a poem praising Lord Vishnu in twelve verses. These are called the Dhruva-stuti.

The pleased Vishnu granted the young boy his wish, bestowing on him the status of a star, a celestial body, untouched by the world in every way.

Vishnu turned the seven rishis who had protected Dhruva on earth into stars, too. He placed these stars around Dhruva Tara, the unmoving Pole Star, around which the seven stars move slowly as the Big Dipper asterism of the Ursa Major constellation, also known as the Great Bear constellation.

In Ramayana, there is a verse: *Dhruvam Sarve Pradakshinam.* It refers to Dhruva or Dhruvam as the Pole Star and the seven sages or the Saptarishis, the sun, the moon, and all the visible planets offering *pradakshinam* or circumambulation to it. This is symbolic of both the exalted status of Dhruva as well as the belief that the lord resides in the heart of his devotees.

Sharvara and Shyama,
Canis Major and Canis Minor

Sharvara and Shyama, the two ferocious, four-eyed dogs associated with Yama are known to the world as Canis Major and Canis Minor constellations. Canis Major lies in the southern celestial hemisphere. It means 'greater dog' in Latin. Canis Minor is a small constellation in the northern celestial hemisphere. Its name in Latin means 'lesser dog.'

These translations might be puzzling for some, but their connection lies in mythology and symbolic representation. The shape of the Canis Major constellation resembles that of a big dog, while Canis Minor's shape resembles that of a smaller dog, and both these hunting dogs follow the hunter named Orion. In Greek Mythology, the mythical hunter Orion is chasing a hare – which is represented by the Lepus constellation that lies in the northern sky, literally at Orion's feet – giving credence to the story that the hunter along with his two dogs is pursuing the hare.

Both the Canis Major and Minor constellations are a part of the Orion family of constellations. They come under the category of eighty-eight modern constellations.

Canis Major also boasts of the beautiful Milky Way passing through it.

Canis Major, Canis Minor, and Canes Venatici (the hunting dogs) are the three constellations in the sky named after dogs.

In Hindu mythology, Canis Major and Canis Minor were considered Sharvara (also called Sabala) and Shyama, the two watchdogs of Yama, the god of death. These dogs spend their time guarding the gates of the underworld. Early Vedic tradition mentions Sabala, the spotted one, and Shyama, the dark or the black one, doing their master's (Yama's) bidding by bringing the souls of the dead into the afterlife called Naraka or the Purgatory and guarding them there at Yama's city Yamapura.

The two dogs of Yama are as fearsome as their master. Sharvara and Shyama can be described as dusk and dawn. It could also mean that death can happen anytime. These dogs are mentioned in a section of the Rig Veda called Yamasukta. The dogs' names are mentioned in a prayer to Yama, beseeching the lord of the underworld to request his dogs to protect the dead and ease their passage to his palace. Souls of the dead must get past the watchdogs in order to join their ancestors, the pitrs, who are already present there.

As only one dog can see at a time, they each have two pairs of eyes, so as to do a thorough job. When Lord Yama travels on his buffalo, Sharvara and Shyama walk alongside.

Though the dogs are mentioned in the Atharva Veda too, there a different role is attributed to them. They are considered messengers of Yama, entrusted with the task of looking for individuals who are supposed to die.

There is yet another version that considers the two dogs as a group of asuras called Kalakanjas. These Kalakanjas were constructing a stairway to heaven. What an impossible feat that only asuras forever in search of the good things can think of! As this stairway grew taller, Indra pulled out one of its bricks to put a stop to this unwanted escalator. This structure crashed, just like a house of cards, sending the asuras tumbling down in a heap. Most of the asuras transformed into spiders to prevent damage to their bodies, especially their bones, and landed safely. But the two asuras at the top weren't so lucky. They ended up turning into dogs, either their transforming skills were not up to par or perhaps it all went horribly wrong. They also had a double whammy when they were cursed to guard Yama's kingdom forever. Now whether they considered that a blow or not, no one has asked the dogs, as no one has ever returned from the land of the dead.

These two dogs command a lot of respect as no one wants to earn the wrath of the god of death by being rude to his pets.

Svana,
Sirius, the Dog Star

Sirius, also known as the Dog Star, is the brightest star in the night sky. Why is it called Dog Star? Because it is situated in the Canis Major (Greater Dog) constellation. Because of its immense brightness, Sirius was well-recognized and well-known by the ancients, and it became an object of veneration for them.

The name Sirius means 'glowing,' 'sparkling,' or 'scorching' in Greek. The ancient Greeks and Romans considered Sirius as the harbinger of the intense summer heatwaves. They also credited this star as being instrumental in intensifying the sun's heat.

In the stories from our epics, Sirius is considered Svana, the dog who followed Yudhisthira, the eldest of the five Pandavas, during his final journey.

After the Kurukshetra War was over, the Pandavas regained their kingdom of Hastinapur and ruled prosperously over it for many years. One day, leaving the kingdom in the capable hands of their descendants (great-grandchildren), the five Pandavas and Draupadi renounced their throne, their kingdom, and ventured on their ultimate adventure – the

Mahaprasthana or the great departure, to meet their maker. This decision was also due to the fact that their friend, guide, and mentor Krishna had left the world several years back.

They crossed lands and seas until they arrived at the base of the Himalayas, with Yudhishthira leading the small group. As they started climbing the snowy mountain, a dog joined them, walking beside Yudhishthira.

As they started climbing higher and higher, spending days and nights on the tall mountain, one by one, they began to die. Draupadi was the first one to collapse.

Bheema asked Yudhishthira the reason why such a compassionate woman like Draupadi died. Yudhishthira replied that though the five Pandavas were her husbands, Draupadi was partial towards Arjuna. This was the reason for her fall.

Sahadeva was the next one to collapse. When Bheema asked Yudhishthira the reason for it, he was told that the reason for Sahadeva's fall was his pride about his intelligence.

As they climbed further and further, Nakula, Arjuna, and Bheema collapsed. The reason for their deaths were: Nakula's pride in his looks; Arjuna's overconfidence due to his skill in archery; and Bheema's arrogance due to his strength. Bheema's gluttony too had contributed to his fall.

Only the dog trailed Yudhishthira silently, like a faithful shadow. When Yudhishthira finally reached the gates of heaven after a long and tiring journey, the dog was at his heels. Opening the gate of heaven, Indra welcomed Yudhishthira, asking him to leave the dog behind. Yudhishthira refused to walk through the golden gates without Svana, the dog, who had been his faithful companion throughout the journey, even when his brothers and his wife had left him due to their weaknesses.

Seeing Yudhishthira's determination, the dog transformed into its original form – the god of Dharma, whose intention was to test the eldest of the Pandavas, and for that purpose he had assumed the form of a dog. Indra recognized the pure feelings and the integrity Yudhishthira was known for. He welcomed both into heaven and that's where they live. Yudhishthira in heaven and the dog Svana in the sky as Sirius the Dog Star.

One can never doubt the faithfulness of a canine, and Svana proved himself by not leaving Yudhishthira alone in his last journey and was rewarded for it.

Saptarishis,
Big Dipper Asterism

The Big Dipper asterism, also called the Plough, is part of the third-largest constellation called the Ursa Major. It is one of the most easily recognizable asterisms in the sky.

Let me explain what an asterism means: an asterism is a pattern or a group of stars visible in the sky, observed either with the naked eye or through a telescope. An asterism can be a simple shape formed by a handful of stars or it can be a complicated pattern made by many stars covering a large part of the sky. The Big Dipper asterism comprises seven bright stars. Four of these stars make the shape of a bowl or the body, while the other three form the shape of a handle or the head.

It is also one of the largest pattern of stars in the northern hemisphere. It has a unique feature: it never goes below the horizon. Its brightest star is Alioth, which is about 102 times brighter than the sun.

For centuries, the Big Dipper asterism has been used as a navigational tool. The reason is that two of its stars, Dubhe and Merak, form a pointer, which is a straight line leading to the North Star, Polaris. The Big Dipper was also utilized as a celestial clock as it rotates counterclockwise around the north celestial pole.

The Big Dipper has several other names: the Plough, the Great Wagon, or Saptarishi mandal.

To meet the Saptarishis, we need to visit an open-air classroom on the banks of the Kanti Sarovar near the Kedarnath Temple. These Saptarishis who became a part of the Big Dipper asterism were the studious seven who did their teacher proud. The glacial lake had frozen, an icy wind blew all around. But the moment the cold and harsh wind approached the place where the teacher sat surrounded by his seven students, it lowered its intensity, tiptoeing, as it didn't want the seven students to get distracted from absorbing the lessons the teacher was teaching and the knowledge he was imparting.

Without desks and chairs, pencils and notebooks, the studious seven soaked in all the knowledge of the yogic science, the different aspects of yoga, the asanas, pranayama that would enhance their spiritual life, meditation that would take them deeper into their spiritual goals. They were particularly interested in the science of inner transformation that the master was discussing. When the teacher spoke, pearls of wisdom dropped from his lips, when he fell silent, gold dust of knowledge telepathically moved towards the students' mind, penetrating their thoughts and illuminating their understanding.

This was a classroom with a difference. Never before had such a teacher walked on earth, never after would such students grace any school. The teacher was Adiyogi (Lord

Shiva's Yogi avatar) and the super seven were the Saptarishis – the seven enlightened, learned, and wise rishis born from Lord Brahma's thoughts and mind. Treated equivalent to the devas due to their power, they were Vashishta, Atri, Marichi, Pulaha, Kratu, Pulastya, and Angiras. Praised in the Vedas and other holy scriptures, the Saptarishis were an exalted lot.

After their learning was over, Adiyogi asked them to go in seven different directions to pass on this knowledge to the rest of humanity. Armed with this knowledge of yoga and their understanding of Brahman, the divine consciousness that pervades the entire universe, these revered sages spread this knowledge among the rest of humanity so that humankind would benefit from it.

These seven holy sages performed severe tapasya and accumulated yogic power that gave them extremely long lifespans and a semi-immortal status. These star sages had a huge fan following, with powerful kings, other rishis, commoners, and even the demigods in awe of their knowledge and power.

It is said that the Saptarishis live in the sky as a constellation called the Saptarishi mandal (the seven prominent stars) or the Big Dipper asterism.

Let's meet the studious seven, though you've read about them earlier in the nakshatras.

Rishi Vashishta, one of the most well-known of the saptarishis, emerged from the creator Brahma's breath. He was the royal guru of King Dasharatha. When Dasharatha performed the Putrakameshti Yagna for begetting sons who

The position of four of the stars (Megrez, Phecda, Merak, and Dubhe) resembles a plough and the three (Alkaid, Mizar-Alcor, and Alioth) look like its long tail. Another star Alcor, close to the Big Dipper, especially close to Mizar, is known as Arundhati star. Arundhati is Vashishta's wife, famous for her loyalty to her husband. The two stars Mizar and Alcor form a double star, the first double star to be discovered. People of the medieval age believed that the star Alkaid had magical properties.

Mizar (Zeta Ursae Majoris) – Vashishta
Alioth (Epsilon Ursae Majoris) – Angiras
Megrez (Delta Ursae Majoris) – Atri
Phecda (Gamma Ursae Majoris) – Pulastya
Merak (Beta Ursae Majoris) – Pulaha
Dubhe (Alpha Ursae Majoris) – Kratu
Alkaid (Eta Ursae Majoris) – Marichi

would become heir to his kingdom, it was Rishi Vashishta who suggested that the Putrakameshti Yagna be conducted.

With a name that means unmatched brilliance, he is said to have conquered all his negative traits such as desire, anger, envy, pride, stinginess, attachment, and jealousy. He is considered one of the oldest sages, revered by young and old alike. This sage had trikala jnana – the ability to see the past, present, and future – that placed him high in the world of rishis. Wouldn't it be lovely to have such a vision?

Vashishta is one teacher every student of that time wanted. His wife was Arundhati, a woman renowned for her devotion to her husband.

The second student was Maharishi Atri. He manifested from Brahma's eye. His devotion was unparalleled as was his integrity and dedication. His wife, Anasuya Devi, matched him in piety. Rishis Atri's life is said to have traversed several yugas. He is mentioned in both the Ramayana as well as the Mahabharata.

The third of the studious seven was Rishi Angiras, who had his own fandom. Born from Brahma's mouth, he was a force to reckon with. Angiras is also one of the ten Prajapatis Brahma created to procreate and populate the world. Angiras was supposed to have written the very first verse of the Rig Veda, a hymn to Agni. Angiras had two wives, Surupa and Smriti. From all his children, Brihaspati is the most well-known.

Another student who sat rapt in the open-air classroom was Rishi Pulastya. He was born from the ear (*karna*) of Brahma. He took the words of the creator to heart and went on to produce several species to fill the world. He had Vishrava and Agastya from his wife Manini. With his wife Priti, he had several Vanaras. With Havirbhu he had the Gandharvas, and with Swayamvara, the Kinnaras. His son Rishi Vishrava had several children. The more well-known among them were Kubera, the god of wealth, Ravana, Kumbhakarna, Vibhishana, and a daughter Surpanakha.

Another student sitting in the open-air classroom was Pulaha. He emerged from Brahma's navel. Pulaha married Kshama, one of Daksha Prajapati's daughters. Pulaha's hermitage hosted King Bharata (son of king Dushyanta and queen Shakuntala).

The next rishi on the student list is Kratu. He can stake a claim to being one of dearest sons of Lord Brahma, born from the creator's hand. Kratu was also the son-in-law of Prajapati Daksha, married to his daughter Sannati (Santhati). But for all his high status, Kratu was not spared during the destruction at Prajapati Daksha's yagna. Shiva, enraged by his wife's self-immolation, wreaked havoc at the site. He mutilated Kratu's male organ.

The Bhagavata Purana mentions that after Kratu's organ was restored by Shiva, he married Prajapati Daksha's daughter Sannati and they had sixty thousand sons, known as the Valakhilyas or Balakhilyas. These were the pygmy sages, as small as the joint of a thumb. The Valakhilyas were chaste, pious, and as radiant as the sun. They all had the luminance of the sun in their body and also energized themselves by soaking in the rays of the sun for their daily energy.

Another student who made Adiyogi proud was Rishi Marichi (or Mareechi), born from Brahma's mind. *Marichi* means a 'beam' or 'ray of light.' The Vedic scriptures give Marichi the position of one of the seven types of storm gods, making him the chief of the Maruts, who are known as the shining ones. Rishi Marichi was known for his profound wisdom and knowledge. He played a huge role in guiding humanity in both worldly and spiritual matters.

Marichi's expertise in meditation and penances was unmatched. He had immense spiritual energy. This controlling deity of the heavenly spaces had a whole lot of illustrious descendants, who lent their might to the family name, taking the glorious legacy forward. Marichi's family tree boasts of some celestial superstars, especially his son Kashyapa. Kashyapa not only inherited his father's right of creation, but he was also considered a Prajapati by many. Marichi's great grandson was Manu, the first man, the father of humanity.

The Saptarishis are revered as Manasaputras – mind-born sons of Brahma. They are believed to reside beneath Dhruva loka. These revered sages keep the sacred waters of the Ganges on the tufts of hair on their heads. After their life on earth, the Saptarishis rose to the hallowed position of stars in the Big Dipper asterism of the Great Bear constellation.

SELECT BIBLIOGRAPHY

Bhagwath, Arvind, *Mythology of Nakshatras*, PDF uploaded on 25 May 2023 https://www.scribd.com/document/773542035/MythologyofNakshatras

DiCara, Vic (Vraja Kishor). *27 Stars, 27 Gods, The Astrological Mythology of Ancient India*. Createspace Independent Pub (29 December 2012).

Murty, Sudha. *The Man from the Egg: Unusual Tales about the Trinity*. Puffin, 2017.

Murty, Sudha. *The Serpent's Revenge: Unusual Tales from the Mahabharata*. Puffin, 2016.

Nayak, Satyarth. *Mahagatha: 100 Tales from the Puranas*. HarperCollins Publishers India, 2022.

Pai, Roopa. *The Vedas and Upanishads for Children*. Hachette India, 2019.

Patnaik, Devdutt. *Stars and Planets: Gods in the Sky*. Penguin Books India, 2016.

Sadhguru and Subramaniam, Arundhati. *Adiyogi: The Source of Yoga*. Haper Element, 2017.

Shastri, J.L., *The Shiva Purana*. Motilal Banarsidass, 1950. https://archive.org/details/dli.bengal.10689.20655/page/n447/mode/2up

Trivedi, Prash. *The Book of Nakshatras: A Comprehensive Treatise on 27 Constellations*. Sagar Publications, 2009.

Wilson, H.H. *The Vishnu Purana*. Wisdom Library, 1840. https://www.wisdomlib.org/hinduism/book/vishnu-purana-wilson

Last but not the least, the Internet, where I read many articles written by astrologers.

ACKNOWLEDGEMENTS

This was the most difficult book I have written so far. There were several moments of despair in the year and a half that I took to write and rewrite this book, several times. The topic was such that there were not many books to research from. The few books I could manage to get my hands on, differed widely in their perspective. The more books I read, the more awestruck I felt about the mystical world of nakshatras, a word unfamiliar to many, to me too. As I delved deeper and deeper into my research, the book slowly started taking shape.

Huge thanks to Vatsala Kaul Banerjee for sending this project my way and for starting this book's journey.

Having an editor like Sanya Verma made working on this book a bit easy. She was open to all my suggestions, her feedback was like gold and her patience was as vast as the world of nakshatras. She read the innumerable drafts I wrote, because the book was in a tantrum-throwing mood, refusing to follow my instructions and often running away from me. Thank you, Sanya, for being a dream editor. Your words of encouragement were instrumental in the book taking shape.

Surina Jain, for her immaculate copy editing. Surina was so meticulous that I had to triple check all my facts before putting them in the book. Thank you.

Sonali Zohra, thank you for the stunning cover.

Vibha Surya, thank you for bringing the gods and the symbols to life through your illustrations.

My dad Motilal Chhabria, for guiding me from the world beyond the clouds and urging me on, every time I felt I just couldn't write this book. My mom Sheela Chhabria, for her enthusiasm to read the book and for her constant motivation and belief that I could write this book. For listening excitedly to the bits and pieces I read to her. Her constant encouragement and support means a lot. My Guru, Sadguru Mata Amritanandamayi Devi, for her blessings. Ganesha, for lighting my path.

Prasanna Aunty and Gopalkrishnan Uncle, for guiding me towards the right people and the right books for research.